The Last of the Fathers

THOMAS MERTON

The Last of the Fathers

SAINT BERNARD OF CLAIRVAUX AND THE ENCYCLICAL LETTER, *DOCTOR MELLIFLUUS*

GREENWOOD PRESS, PUBLISHERS
WESTPORT, CONNECTICUT

TO ETIENNE GILSON

CONTENTS

Preface

Saint Bernard of Clairvaux, the "Last of the Fathers of the Church," died in his monastery in Burgundy on the twentieth of August, 1153. One of the dominant figures in the history of the Church, and by all odds the greatest in his own century, he had tremendous influence on the political, literary, and religious life of Europe. Yet like other complex and many-sided characters, he suffered a rapid and disconcerting fragmentation at the hands of his own fame. Perhaps he was too great to be remembered in his entirety. It has ended with history celebrating one side of him, theology another, piety a third, his own monastic Order a fourth. At one time we see him a reformer, a preacher of Crusades; at another as the intransigent accuser of heresy; again as the ardent preacher whose devotion to the Humanity of Christ led to the formation of a whole new school of spirituality—the so-called *devotio moderna*, of which the principal monument is "The Imitation of Christ." Finally we see him as the lean ascetic who had almost forgotten how to eat. The eighth centenary of his death has seemed a propitious time to bring these fragments together, and nothing has been more effective in doing so than the encyclical, *Doctor Mellifluus*, issued at the Vatican by His Holiness Pope Pius XII on Whitsunday of 1953.

[9]

Preface

Not the least of the services that have been performed by this publication is the return to a whole and integral picture of Saint Bernard, with emphasis not on the secondary and accidental phases of his career, but on the most important thing of all: his sanctity, his union with God, his conformity to Christ by perfect charity, and his teaching inspired as much by his study of Scripture and the Fathers as by his own experience of mystical union.

A papal encyclical is never a document of merely transient importance. It is always a concise and fully authoritative summary of the teaching accepted and approved by the Church on a given subject. *Doctor Mellifluus* tells us what Saint Bernard means to the Church. It presents him to us as a Doctor of the Church, therefore as an organ of the teaching Church and a sure witness of Christian tradition.

Not all the Doctors of the Church enjoy the high-sounding official titles that the schools have attached to the names of some of them. The fashion of giving every doctor a "title" goes back to the thirteenth century, when there was a great confusion of "Universal Doctors," "Irrefragable Doctors," and "Sublime Doctors" in the faculties of the great universities. Not all of them were Doctors of the Church, by any means. Only a few of the titles are still commonly known—Saint Thomas Aquinas is the "Angelic Doctor," Saint Bonaventure the "Seraphic Doctor," Duns Scotus the "Subtle Doctor." * I do not know when

* A later generation has paid tribute to Duns Scotus' defense of the Immaculate Conception by giving him the title "Doctor Marianus." This title is also accorded by some to Saint Bernard.

Preface

Saint Bernard got to be known as the Mellifluous Doctor. Not in the twelfth century, surely; it sounds like a more recent invention. What it means is "The Doctor whose teaching is as sweet as honey," or more literally, the "Doctor-flowing-with-honey."

The title is significant, after all, because Saint Bernard is sometimes regarded as an angry character. He was not so. There were, indeed, times in his life when he had to be angry in the cause of justice. And he could be splendidly angry. But his doctrine is much less austere and forbidding than that of other writers of his age. He seems extraordinarily gentle when compared with a great reformer of the tenth century, the Camaldolese hermit Saint Peter Damian. Indeed, Saint Bernard seems to have struck an altogether new note of hope and encouragement in medieval spirituality, and it is no exaggeration to attribute to him the current of sweetness and joy that was to become in Francis of Assisi "a stream of the river making the city of God joyful" (Psalm 45:5).

We ourselves are just emerging from a time in which sweetness has been overdone, and perhaps we do not find the concept too attractive. Let us not, by any means, associate the sweetness of Saint Bernard with the insipid sentimentality and bad taste of a piety that is untrue. Sentimentality is, after all, only a fake. It is a meretricious pretense of emotion, and has nothing to do with genuine human feeling, except that it sometimes gets itself accepted as a passable imitation. The falsity of this kind of piety lies precisely in the fact that it appeals to nothing except the emotions, and in so doing it fails even to arouse a mature and integrally human emotional response. The preaching of Bernard of Clairvaux does have emotional repercussions. Let us not be so foolish as to deny the emotions a part either in our life or in our religion. But for Bernard emotion is never the end in view. It would be quite false to suppose that the deep and rich religious experience everywhere reflected in Saint Bernard's writings and in his life was something that had been sought for its own sake. The sweetness of Bernard remains clean because he seldom stops to think subjectively about sweetness. It is not at all self-conscious. It does not even spring up from any source within Bernard himself. It is an overflow from the goodness and mercy and charity of God.

This encyclical brings out quite clearly that the "honey" in the doctrine of Bernard is not the cloying sweetness of a soul enclosed within itself, but the clean, fresh sweetness of the fields and the forest. It is the breath of true life, of divine life, of supernatural charity, and of the Holy Spirit. It is the happy vitality of a soul made alive by self-sacrifice, and the joy of a heart that lives no longer for itself but for others, and above all for God. In short, the "honey" of Saint Bernard's doctrine is nothing else but the spiritual peace distilled in the silence of the

monastic life. The essentially monastic character of
all Saint Bernard's writing is what gives it a very special quality of its own. It is this character that especially recommends his books to us now, in an age
that is proving itself hungry for the spiritual prov-
ender that has lain hidden, all these centuries, in
Christian monasticism.

What is the monastic life? It is the life of those
who have left the "world" with its desires and its
ambitions in order to devote themselves entirely to
seeking God. It is, according to Saint Bernard, a
paradise of charity in which it is fully possible for
the Christian to live out his baptismal vocation and
follow, without half-measures, the Gospel of Christ.
It is first of all a contemplative life, but actually all
forms of Christian living find a place for themselves
in the microcosm of the monastic community. Many
in the cloister will be penitents above all. Others will
serve their brethren with active charity. Still others
will be contemplatives in the truest sense of the
word, men of interior solitude and mystical prayer.
Finally, that most complete of all vocations, the union
of action and contemplation in the care of souls, also
finds a place in the monastery and may in certain ex-
ceptional cases even extend beyond the enclosure.*

Nourishing our souls with the substance of Saint
Bernard's doctrine we will be able to gain a more
just and better proportioned idea of the full mean-

* See our article "Action and Contemplation in Saint Bernard" in
Collectanea, O.C.R., January, July, 1953, April, 1954.

ing of monasticism. It is indeed the very completeness and integration of the Cistercian life which gave Bernard his own peculiar strength and universality. Reading him, we may dare to hope for a return to that integral spirit, in so far as such a return may be possible in our time.

Doctor Mellifluus is without any doubt one of the most interesting and significant documents issued by His Holiness Pope Pius XII. The importance of its message has not yet received the attention it deserves. When the encyclical came out, there were brief reports of it in the Catholic press, but at the time of writing this preface no complete English text has been printed in the United States. It seems fitting that it should now receive a wide dissemination, for nothing could be more timely than its timeless appeal for a return to genuine Christian charity, nourished by a deep interior life, sustained by contemplation, and bearing fruit not so much in material works as in true love for other men.

The importance of this encyclical lies above all in its practicality. Pope Pius XII makes use of the doctrine of Saint Bernard to bring the highest spiritual perfection within reach of all Christians, whether they be living in the cloister or in the world. And he shows us that the Gospel of Christ, which was preached to all men by the Savior and His Apostles, must still remain a living reality in the lives of all. Indeed it must be the one reality upon which our lives are entirely centered if life is to retain its significance.

Preface

In order that the encyclical might be better understood, it was decided that someone should write a brief commentary on it, adding at the same time a few pages on Saint Bernard's life and on his written works. It has been my singular privilege to perform this task, which I should have hesitated to undertake but for the desire of my Superiors, and which I could not have brought to a conclusion without the benevolent encouragement of His Eminence Peter Cardinal Fumasoni-Biondi, former Apostolic Delegate to Washington and Cardinal Protector of the Cistercians. I take this occasion to thank His Eminence for the prefatory letter which he has graciously permitted us to include in these pages, along with another letter which we owe to the paternal kindness of the Most Reverend Dom M. Gabriel Sortais, the Father General of our Order.

Letter from the Cardinal Protector

Into a world where fear and distrust run as a seemingly overpowering force, where men seek to rely on force and human strategy, our Holy Father, Pius XII, has injected once more the Christian call to hope and trust and reliance on divine love and strategy.

The great exponent of divine love, Saint Bernard of Clairvaux, is recalled to our memory in this encyclical, *Doctor Mellifluus.* As Cardinal Protector of the Sacred Order of Cistercians, and as an old friend of the Trappist Cistercians, I rejoice at this revival of the teachings of Saint Bernard, the great defender of the Church.

Our everyday world has great need of Saint Bernard and we sincerely hope that all of good will shall read and meditate on the teachings here contained. The teachings of Saint Bernard can be a beacon leading us, one and all, to love, for we were made to love, not to fear. "God is love," yesterday, today and forever.

Peter, Cardinal Fumasoni-Biondi
Prefect, S. Congregation of Propaganda Fide

Letter from the Abbot General

With all my heart I bless your plan to publish the encyclical *Doctor Mellifluus*, which His Holiness Pius XII has just written about our blessed Father Saint Bernard.

The soul of our great saint is depicted in this document with such delicacy, such finesse, and such accuracy! In making this encyclical known, you will help your fellow Americans to get some idea of the spiritual ideal that was lived so intensely by our blessed Father—that ideal which was the secret of his influence and of his spiritual ascendancy both among his sons at Clairvaux and in all the world of his time.

I hope that very many souls will be attracted and captivated by the doctrine of the holy Abbot of Clairvaux, and that they will seek only to give God a greater place in their lives and to meet the demands of divine love with a generous reply. God in His turn will not fail to pour out many graces upon them, and may perhaps call them to the sublime favor of union with Himself.

May Our Lady bring you my blessing and increase it a hundredfold.

Fr. M. Gabriel Sortais, O.C.S.O.
Abbot of Citeaux

1

THE MAN AND
THE SAINT

T HE ENIGMA of sanctity is the temptation and often the ruin of historians. This is all the truer of a saint like Bernard of Clairvaux who dominated the whole history of his time. Sanctity is born of conflict—of contradictories resolved into union. The historian is tempted to see in Bernard only the struggle between social and cultural forces which found in him their incarnation: for Bernard contained the whole twelfth century in himself. That is to say that he embodied and united in himself two other great ages, and lived the transition between them. His life, his career, religious and political, were the working out in himself, but for his contemporaries as well as for himself, of all their common problems. I do not say he achieved their solution, for no age, no generation, no one man, see the solution of all their problems. There were many things in which Saint Bernard failed. His failures were as great and as significant and ultimately as constructive as his successes. Almost everything that he did had tremendous effect in shaping the course of history.

It is not enough to see in Bernard the union of Romanesque and Gothic, the transition from Saint Gregory VII to Saint Francis of Assisi—from the tenth century to the thirteenth. A brilliant but insufficient explanation of the tremendous work done by Saint Bernard attributes his genius and his energy and his sanctity to a dialectical tension between these two great spiritual forces which confronted one another in his soul. This theory will not serve. Yet the forces were there, and we must take them into account.

On one hand, Bernard was a Burgundian nobleman, a warrior born for knighthood or for prelacy. The walls and towers of the monastic basilica of Cluny were rising massively into the sky when he was born in 1090 in a castle not far from Dijon. Cluny was a living expression of the great, unified, and reformed ecclesiastical structure that had been left by Pope Gregory VII, at his death five years before. Cluny meant power, authority, centralization, law. Its grandeur, the lavishness of its liturgy, the vastness of its monastic empire were the outward expression of the rule of Christ the King in His Church, of the penetration of His Kingship into every department of human life and culture. The Cluny of Saint Hugh and the Rome of Saint Gregory VII belonged to a world that believed Peter had two swords: one his temporal, the other his spiritual power. No one was surprised that he wielded both.

At the same time a new generation was being born. Feudalism was ready to fall apart, and the time of the communes and the guilds and the cathedrals and the universities was at hand. The young Bernard of Fontaines, who might have won himself a high place in the Church, or fame in her schools, refused to be famous or great, renounced his inheritance and his opportunities, and headed for a solitude which the towers of Cluny could only disdain. He feared to serve in the court of the great King because he felt that he was called to something much greater than power. He believed in the Christ *Pantocrator*, but felt that this great Lord would reveal Himself far differently in the forest of Citeaux. The One he sought in poverty, silence, and solitude was the *Verbum Sponsus*, the God who manifests Himself not only to the whole world as its King and Judge, but to the humble and solitary soul as its Bridegroom, in the secrecy of prayer.

Hence there was in Bernard a stronger attraction, a more powerful current which carried him away from the liturgical splendors of Cluny as well as from the subtleties of the schools. It was the current of mysticism, asceticism, liberty, spirituality, personalism which was already beginning to branch out in so many directions: one branch leading to a Francis of Assisi, another to the heresy of Albi.

Saint Bernard seems to have thought it possible to renounce everything of the first element in his soul, and live entirely by the second. Things were not to be so simple. His very reputation as a mystic, an ascetic, a miracle worker, a saint made it impossible for him to avoid becoming a great churchman, a defender of authority, of law, of the papacy, a man of God in politics, a preacher of Crusades. More than that: his spirit could never be one of mere individualistic piety. It was because he was at once so much a person, and so much a mystic, that Bernard was also essentially a man of the Church—*Vir Ecclesiae*.

We shall glance presently at some details of his tremendously active life. Although the tension between these two apparently conflicting powers does not account for that life, or for its achievements, or for its sanctity, it was most certainly a factor in his sanctification, because, as we have said, all sanctity is born of conflict.

To explain the sanctity of Bernard by enumerating the works and struggles and problems he had to confront is like explaining the sanctity of Thérèse of Lisieux by saying that one of her Sisters splashed dirty water on her in the laundry and another distracted her with a noisy rosary during mental prayer. There are in all the saints two other opposed elements to be reconciled and united: the human and the divine. This conflict counters the other, cuts across it at right angles, and even lifts it upwards bodily into a new dimension. But here everything takes place in mystery. We cannot see what happens, because no man can see into another man's soul. He can barely see a little into his own!

When talking of Saint Bernard, we must necessarily talk more about what we know than about what we cannot know. But in pointing out the visible accidents and effects on the surface of a deep invisible life of sanctity, let us always remember that what is not seen is the essential. Everything that falls outside the periphery of the central mystery, everything that can be seen clearly in the life of a saint is actually of little consequence unless it somehow be a sign of his inward sanctity. More precisely, the thoughts and acts and virtues of a saint are not wonderful in themselves, but they are meant to be deeply significant flashes sent forth from the dark bosom of the mystery of God. For the saint does not represent himself, or his time, or his nation: he is a sign of God for his own generation and for all generations to come.

Furthermore, sanctity is supernatural life. The saints not only have life, but they give it. Their sanctity is best known to those who have received life from them. The men of Bernard's time had no doubt of what they were getting from him. He cast fire on the earth wherever he went. The power of Bernard was more than the influence of genius or the persuasive efficacy of heroic virtue: it was charismatic. God worked in him, and worked such wonders that men knew it was God they had seen at work, not man. The grace of the God who had possession of this frail man burst into flame in the hearts of all who heard him speak.

It is for us to understand Saint Bernard's sanctity not merely by studying his history, but by perceiving something of its life-giving effect. It is precisely the aim of a papal encyclical to help us to do this. That is why *Doctor Mellifluus* treats Saint Bernard above all as a *Doctor* and a *"Father"* of the Church, rather than as a great figure in the history of his own time.

The liturgy of Saint Bernard's feast in the Cistercian missal and breviary show how firmly the Church believes in the life-giving power still exercised, in the Communion of Saints, by those whom she reveres as Fathers and Doctors. Like Bernard himself, she teaches that Christ communicates Himself to men through the ministerial action of His saints not only in their own lifetime but also after their death.* So the monks chant in one of their responsories, addressing Saint Bernard: "Thou hast entered into the powers of the Lord and now made more powerful as intercessor, obtain for us a share in the light and sweetness which you now enjoy!" (*"Introisti in potentias Domini, et jam potentior ad impetrandum, fac nos ejus qua frueris lucis suavitatisque participes."*) †

It would therefore be useless for us to attempt, in a short space, to list even a few of Saint Bernard's great achievements, to trace even a broad outline of his travels in the service of God, to describe his monastic reforms, his new foundations, his interventions in the affairs of kings, bishops, and popes. But we must give some idea of his life and character. The easiest way of doing so is to look at him at three decisive points in his career. We shall open the book of his life at three places only: first, in 1115, when he is a young abbot of twenty-five; second in 1124, a little beyond the halfway mark in his life, at the turning point

---

* See the article Bernard, Saint, by Dom Anselme le Bail, O.C.S.O., in *Dictionnaire de Spiritualité*, vol. I, col. 1491.

† *Cistercian Breviary*, Matins of the Feast of Bernard, 9th Responsory.

of his career; and finally in 1145 when Bernard is, practically speaking, Pope.

Saint Bernard had saved the life of a new monastery, Citeaux, by entering it with thirty companions in 1112. The foundation, which had seemed ready to expire in 1111, was strong enough to found three other monasteries in 1114 and 1115. In June of 1115, shortly after the foundation of Morimond, Bernard was sent out by Stephen Harding to start a monastery in a sunny valley in the Langres plateau, on the borders of Burgundy and Champagne. The place was to become famous as Clairvaux, the "Valley of Light"; famous because of Bernard its abbot, because of the saints who lived there, because of the life they lived, because of the God whom they had found. Clairvaux and Bernard both meant one thing above all: the great twelfth-century revival of mysticism, a spiritual renaissance which had its effects in all the other renaissances of the time. For Bernard was to influence everything from politics to the *roman courtois* and the whole humanistic trend to "courtly love." He left his mark on schools of spirituality, on Gregorian chant, on the clerical life, and on the whole development of Gothic architecture and art. One of the signs of a spiritual revival that is really spiritual is that it affects every kind of life and activity around it, inspires new kinds of art, awakens a new poetry and a new music, even makes lovers speak to one another in a new language and think about one another with a new kind of respect.

But in 1115, Clairvaux is not yet famous. Bernard

lives there with his twelve companions, in little wooden shacks under the trees of the forest. Bernard has just been ordained priest and blessed as abbot by the Bishop of Châlons-sur-Marne—the philosopher William of Champeaux. And William will presently get himself delegated by the General Chapter, at Citeaux, to watch over the health of Saint Bernard. The young abbot is already cracking up under the burden of a life in which Cistercian austerity is intensified twentyfold by indigence, lack of food, and by his own implacable asceticism. For the first few years of the new foundation Bernard is forced to live apart from the community in a little hut by himself, which serves as an infirmary. He falls into the hands of a neighborhood quack and nearly dies. But meanwhile postulants and friends begin to come to Clairvaux, and he is sharing with them his meditations on the deep mysteries of the Canticle which he will one day comment on in the chapter hall of a great stone abbey which his monks will soon begin to build. Nothing gives him any reason to believe that his life will be anything but a life of contemplation—disturbed only by the unavoidable cares of his abbatial charge and bearing fruit quietly in the formation and direction of his own monks.

In 1124, nine years later, Clairvaux is still not the great and well-established monastery that one naturally connects with Bernard's name. It is still anxious for security, and the foundations of its future development are being solidly laid by Bernard's two brothers, the cellarers Gerard and Guy. They have

built the donations of pastures and forest land into
a system of granges, or monastic farms kept up by
lay brothers. Clairvaux can, at least, support herself,
and now with the help of a great neighboring prince,
Thibaut of Champagne, the monastery will soon become more prosperous.

Clairvaux has not immediately begun to make
numerous foundations. Of the seventy new monasteries actually to be founded by Saint Bernard, only
three have been established in his first ten years at
Clairvaux. Trois Fontaines came into existence in
October, 1118. One year later, in the fall of 1119,
Fontenay was founded. Foigny, where Saint Bernard
"excommunicated" the flies, came two years after
Fontenay in 1121. It seems as if Saint Bernard hesi-
tates at this time to make many foundations. He certainly resists the spread of the Order into Spain,
refuses to make a foundation in the Holy Land about
this time, holds off from making any more in France
until 1128 when he will see that it is useless to row
against the strong current. He will found Igny in
March and Reigny in September of that year. In the
early thirties he will extend his foundations into
Germany and England (Rievaulx, 1132) and will be
the first to send a Cistercian colony to Spain (Moruela,
1132) in spite of his earlier opposition.

All this has not yet begun to happen in 1124. But
Bernard is nearing the end of the providential "formation" that has prepared him for his great work in
the Church of God. If we say that ten years of ill
health and insecurity and suffering and prayer are

[31]

coming to an end, we do not mean that his health will become good or that his sufferings will not increase or that his life of prayer will not deepen: but he will become strong enough to travel and enter into public life.

Part of his "formation" has been his training in the knowledge of human nature. First, he has had to learn that man is not an angel, that monks still have bodies, and that although he himself has tried not only to mortify his desires, but even to put to death the senses themselves, it is better to remember that man is human and that his human nature is supposed to be divinized by grace, not destroyed by it. Then, too, the Saint who has always been too pure and too spiritual to feel anything of the temptations of the flesh has learned not to be surprised that all men are not exactly like himself. In his own terms, he has learned the value of what he calls the "flight from justice to mercy." He knows that self-denial is incomplete unless it leads to a sympathetic understanding of others, to mercy, to charity; that the "ointment" of fraternal compassion is necessary to show his monks how good and how pleasant it is for brethren to live together in unity (Psalm 132:1).

Now, finally, he is being tested by the sight of great defections from the Order that embodies all his monastic ideals. His young cousin Robert, who had followed him to Citeaux and had been sent with the small colony that established Clairvaux, "apostatized" in 1119 and fled to the relatively easy and opulent life of Cluny. The first in Saint Bernard's collection of letters, and one of the longest, is one to Robert, pleading with him to return to the austerity of Citeaux:

If warm and comfortable furs, if fine and precious cloth, if long sleeves and ample hoods, if dainty coverlets and soft woolen shirts make a saint, why do I delay and not follow you at once? But these things are comforts for the weak, not the arms of fighting men. They who wear soft raiment are in kings' houses. Wine and white bread, honey-wine and pittances, benefit the body, not the soul. The soul is not fattened out of frying pans. Many monks in Egypt served God a long time without fish. Pepper, ginger, cummin, sage, and all the thousand other spices may please the palate, but they inflame lust. And would you make my safety depend on such things? Will you spend your youth safely among them? Salt with hunger is seasoning enough for a man living soberly and wisely.*

The accents are characteristic of Bernard, especially in the early years at Clairvaux.

But 1125 sees a far more dangerous defection from the Cistercians than the passage of one monk from Citeaux to Cluny. One of the companions of Bernard when he entered Citeaux was Arnold, the first Abbot of Morimond. The two young Cistercians started their abbatial career in the same year, 1115, and had to face the same trials, difficulties, and disappointments. Now, suddenly, news comes that the Abbot of Morimond has vanished from his monastery, taking a few monks with him, and has gone off to settle in the Holy Land without asking any permission. Actually the fugitives will never reach Palestine. Arnold will die in Belgium after ignoring Bernard's

* *The Letters of Saint Bernard of Clairvaux*, translated by Bruno Scott James, Chicago, 1953, p. 8.

letter to him, and the Abbot of Clairvaux will be left with the task of gathering the other monks together and bringing them home. The event is an important one in the life of Saint Bernard and of the Order. Morimond is one cornerstone of the new structure, and there is every reason to fear that with the fall of Arnold the whole Order might collapse. Bernard loses his prior, Gaucher, in the shuffle to set things straight after Arnold's apostasy. Gaucher is sent to replace the departed Abbot. But in a short time Clairvaux is to get one of her greatest priors in exchange for this loss. Godfrey de la Roche will return from Fontenay, where he has been abbot, and will assume this office. He will be one of Saint Bernard's most valuable helpers and supporters in the years of activity soon to come.

These years also find Saint Bernard busy with other Orders. First of all, he has many Benedictine friends. The most intimate of these is William, Abbot of the Black Monks at Saint Thierry, outside Rheims. William has been visiting Clairvaux for some years, and lately he has been insisting that he wants to become a Cistercian. But we must not imagine that Bernard wants all Benedictines to become Cistercians. He is not at all in favor of the change, in this case, and he writes to William:

If I am to say what I think (about your plan), I must tell you that, unless I am mistaken, it is something I could not advise you to attempt and that you could not carry out. Indeed I wish for you what it has for long been no secret to me that you wish for yourself. But putting aside what both of us wish, as it is right we should, is safer for me and more advantageous for you if I advise you as I think God wishes. Therefore I say hold on to what you have, remain where you are, and try to benefit those over whom you rule. Do not try to escape the responsibility of office while you are still able to discharge it for the benefit of your subjects. Woe to you if you rule them and do not benefit them because you shirk the burden of ruling them.*

Another close friend of Saint Bernard is the founder of the Premonstratensian Order, Saint Norbert, the future Bishop of Magdeburg. Since his priestly ordination in the same year as Bernard, Norbert has won himself a great reputation as a preacher and an ascetic. In 1120 he formed a religious community in the diocese of Laon, not too far from Clairvaux. The Bishop of Laon, who presented Norbert with the domain of Premontré, also gave Bernard land on which to found the monastery of Foigny. In 1124, Saint Bernard is present at the installation of the Premonstratensians in the monastery of Saint Martin of Laon, and in this same year Norbert tells the Abbot of Clairvaux that there will soon be a great crisis in the Church. He is prophesying the schism of Anacletus II which will break out in 1130 and which will draw Bernard forth from his cloister into the turmoil of the world.

1124 is probably also the date of Saint Bernard's voyage to Grenoble and the Grande Chartreuse. His friendship with Guigo, or Guy, the legislator and organizer of the Carthusian Order is to be extraordinarily fruitful in both of them. Two remarkable

* *Letters,* p. 128.

literary works will remain as a witness to its fruitfulness: the austere and deep *Meditations* of Guigo, and Saint Bernard's own "Treatise on the Love of God" (*De Diligendo Deo*)—one of the most succinct expressions of the central theme of his mystical theology: union with God by pure love.

Finally, the conversion of Saint Bernard's rather worldly sister, Humbeline, and her entrance into the Benedictine convent of Julley-les-Nonnains also belongs to this period of his life (1122).

If the ideas for his *De Diligendo Deo* are now maturing in his mind, two other major works of the *Doctor Mellifluus* have already been completed. They are the sermons on the Virgin Mother (or Homilies on the Gospel "*Missus Est*") and the treatise on the Degrees of Humility. The sermons on the Blessed Virgin are without doubt among the most beautiful pages to come from Bernard's pen. They constitute a small but complete treatise in Mariology, one of the first of its kind. This is one of the only books Saint Bernard writes not on request or under obedience, but merely because he feels like writing it.

In short, at the end of the first quarter of the twelfth century we find that Saint Bernard and the century are fully prepared to meet one another. He is already known to be a saint, a worker of miracles, and a theologian whose wisdom is more than a matter of learning. He is already so much of an authority that a cardinal will urge him to write his book on the love of God and the Bishop of Sens will ask him for a treatise on the spiritual life for bishops. "Who

are we," exclaims Saint Bernard, "that we should
write for bishops!" Yet he adds, "Who are we that
we should not obey our bishops?" He does not hesitate to obey.

Two more lines and we shall fill in the background
of this sketch and pass on. Saint Bernard is perhaps
not thinking much about the Albigensian heresy, but
already there is much trouble in the south of France.
In the heart of Languedoc, where some of the great
Romanesque basilicas of the age are still bright gold
in their unweathered stone, the heresiarch Peter de
Bruys puts on a surprising and unhappy demonstra-
tion. It is Good Friday, and the scene is at Saint-Gilles-
du-Gard. Peter gathers a crowd in the public square,
heaps up a huge pile of crucifixes and sets them
alight. While the fire is blazing, he starts roasting
some meat in the fire, offering it to the crowd. A riot
breaks out with fighting on all sides. Peter is himself
seized and thrown into the flames, but escapes to continue his work and prepare the way for his successor,
Henry, whom Bernard will confront in 1145.

1145 is the year in which Eugene III ascends the
throne of Peter, to become the first Cistercian pope.
Eugene followed Bernard home from Italy on one of
the Saint's triumphant journeys, in the early thirties.
He lived there for ten years as an obscure and silent
monk. Bernard sent him back to Italy in 1140 to be
Abbot of Clairvaux's thirty-fourth foundation: the
Abbey of Tre Fontane outside Rome. The death of
Lucius II, wounded in the Roman civil war, leaves

Eugene and Bernard to settle the struggles of a whole world: Mohammedans in the East, revolutionaries in Italy, heretics in southern France, trouble everywhere. It seems amusing to us that Bernard has written, in 1143, to his friend Peter the Venerable, Abbot of Cluny:

> I have decided to stay in my monastery and not go out, except once a year for the general chapter of Abbots at Citeaux. Here, supported by your prayers and consoled by your good will, I shall remain for the few days that are left to me in which to fight until the time comes for me to be relieved at my post.*

Bernard also writes to his spiritual son who has now become his spiritual father, Pope Eugene III, and tells him rather bluntly that much work can be spared both of them if the Abbot of Clairvaux can only be allowed to rest in peace in the cloister. "If anyone suggests that more might be put on me, know that as it is I am not equal to supporting what I carry. Inasmuch as you spare me you will spare yourself." †

As a matter of fact 1145 finds Bernard and Eugene on the eve of their greatest and most tragic effort: the second Crusade.

The Crusade is Bernard's work. The singular intensity of his religious idealism appears here in all its strength and all its weakness: for Bernard preaches the Crusade with a sublime disregard for political circumstance. He has so completely committed himself to the principles he believes in that he sees

* *Letters*, p. 375.
† *Letters*, p. 396.

nothing but the principles. The whole practical logic of his argument depends on the assumption that each Crusader will take up the Cross with a faith as pure and ardent as Bernard's own. He simply took it for granted that everyone would embrace his religious principles as he did himself, and put them into practice in a manner worthy of saints.

What was this second Crusade? Fifty years before, in Bernard's childhood, when Citeaux was being founded, the first Crusade had established a strange feudal kingdom of Frankish barons in the Holy Land. Here, in not too well garrisoned castles, and surrounded by hostile and uncomprehending natives, the Franks are not united among themselves. Nor are they on very good terms with the nearest great Christian power: the Empire of Byzantium. Facing them is a powerful Moslem coalition, and in 1144 the Mohammedans, under Ibn al Athir, storm and take the Christian outpost of Edessa. It is an important victory, a religious as well as a political triumph for Islam.

The Franks appeal to Byzantium, without result. In 1145 they are asking for help in Rome. The news arrives in France, and the young King Louis VII, seeing a chance of glory, proposes a Crusade. His proposal is not accepted with any enthusiasm. He turns to Bernard of Clairvaux, asking him to preach a Crusade. Bernard will have nothing to do with it. He formally refuses, adding that he will only undertake the task if commanded by the Pope. So Louis VII turns to Rome, and in 1146 Bernard raises the

standard of the Cross at the Burgundian shrine of
Vezelay.

It is here that we see Bernard, the saint, as a most
provoking enigma, as a temptation, perhaps even as
a scandal. Here the sleeping power of Bernard's
warlike atavism wakes and fights its way to the front
of his life like some smiling Romanesque monster
pushing through the leafage of a pillar's capital in
the cloisters of Cluny. This power, too, is part of
his sanctity. Indeed, although it is the fashion (especially among monks) to say that the Bernard of the
Crusade was not the true Bernard, I am not sure
whether Bernard was not more himself, after all, at
Vezelay than he was at Clairvaux. With his whole
heart undividedly set upon one magnificent religious
principle—the principle of order, of divine authority
communicated to men so that the peace of eternity
might begin to be reflected even in the changing surface of the seas of time—Bernard seems to have paid
little attention to temporal detail.

In any case, we cannot see the "true" Bernard by
dividing him against himself, and the truth is that
the Bernard of Vezelay is the very same man who is
prepared, within a short time, to preach the magnificent last sermons on the Canticle of Canticles, sermons which have nothing to do with war but with
the sublime peace of mystical marriage. The apparent
contradiction between Vezelay and the eighty-fifth
sermon *In Cantica* is beyond comprehension if we
imagine that for Saint Bernard the interior life is
purely a matter of personal, subjective, individual

[40]

union of the soul with God. The interior life is the life
of the whole Church, of the Mystical Body of Christ,
shared by all who are members of that Body. But
the invisible and interior peace of the members among
themselves and with their God is not separable, in
the mind of Bernard, from an exterior and visible
order which reflects the purposes of God in the
world, and which guarantees the effect of His salvific
action upon souls. If Saint Bernard thought that the
way to divine union could only be a way of individual withdrawal from the world, of personal asceticism and recollection, of esoteric techniques, he
would hardly urge thousands of Frenchmen and
Englishmen and Germans to take up arms and fight
Islam, to guarantee the security of Christian Europe
and free access to the Holy Places in Palestine. Need-
less to say, although his conception of the Crusade is
essentially mystical, he certainly does not confuse
military action with contemplative prayer. But he
believes that the Church can call upon the armies of
Christian nations to defend the order established by
God. This is a principle which every Catholic will
accept. The difficulty comes, of course, in determin-
ing just what political set-up, if any, represents the
order established by God. Bernard's handling of the
Crusade surprises us by its apparent neglect of this
most important issue. He seems not to have bothered
with the political details of the problem.

It is easy enough to say that Saint Bernard had a
drastically oversimplified idea of the implications of
the Crusade. We may perhaps be inclined to think

[41]

that he ought to have read the translation of the *Koran* which Peter the Venerable sent him, from Cluny, to study and to refute. Bernard seems to have felt no need to know or to understand anything about Islam: as if knowing the Mohammedans to be "pagans" were to know quite enough. But let us remember that Bernard belongs to the twelfth century, not to the twentieth.

The two ages are poles apart. The one can barely understand the other. Our time is completely pragmatic, totally immersed in practical contingency, and rarely argues from anything but circumstance. Bernard did not feel himself obliged to do anything but act in accordance with his one big principle. If God sees fit to call upon the arms of the Franks to defend His Kingdom, and if the Pope tells Bernard to preach a Crusade then the Abbot of Clairvaux has a divine mission to preach a Crusade. He will confine himself to the strict limits of his mission. He will show men the meaning of the Holy War as he himself sees it, and will try to communicate to them something of his own terrific faith. It is someone else's job to see that the right alliances are made among Christian kings or to foresee that they will be either not made or not kept. As for the Crusaders themselves, it is their part to make the war a Holy War, one which is as much a pilgrimage as a war, one in which they will assure themselves of the promised remission of the punishment due to their sins by living without sin.

What actually happened was that Bernard alone did his job well. The others all failed. The murderers and adventurers who joined themselves to the well-intentioned Crusaders remained, alas, murderers and adventurers. The French continued to be enemies of the Germans, and fought them all the way across Europe. The French King did not find it possible to accept an alliance with Roger of Sicily, which would have insured transport by sea and perhaps would have made the presence of so many Westerners in the Near East less alarming for the Emperor at Byzantium. As it was, the armies of the Cross converged on Constantinople and gave the impression that the capital on the Bosporus was the real objective of their Crusade. Manuel Commenius, the Basileus, did what he could to make sure that there would not be a victorious army of Crusaders returning through the city. That meant, in fact, that he made sure there would be no victorious army. To have been a Holy War, as Saint Bernard conceived it, the Crusade ought at least to have manifested some show of unity among Christians. There was none. The whole history of the campaign is one of treachery and murder. "The promises of God," Bernard was to exclaim, "cannot stand in the way of the rights of His justice." *

It is remarkable that Saint Bernard did not give up with the failure of this Crusade. He was ready to start a new one, and had indeed been named to lead it himself: which he would have done. It is said that the Cistercians intervened, and saw to it that he did

* *De Consideratione,* Bk. II, c. 1; Migne, P.L., 182:745.

not. His energy was irrepressible, miraculous to the end. He seems to have excelled in triumphing over sickness in order to do impossible things. Even in the spring of 1153, when Bernard was on his deathbed, he got up and took to the road because he heard there was a war at Metz. But that was to be his last exploit. He died in his monastery on August 20, 1153, lamented by the whole world of his time. He was canonized by Alexander III in 1174.

2

SAINT BERNARD'S
WRITINGS

IT SEEMS that one of the things Saint Bernard wanted to get away from, when he entered Citeaux, was literary ambition. Profoundly affected by the humanistic renaissance of the twelfth century, his works still bear witness, by their quotations from Ovid, Persius, Horace, Terence, and other classical authors, to the influences he met with when he studied the liberal arts with the canons of Saint Vorles at Chatillon-sur-Seine. He seems to have become afraid of poetry and rhetoric, and to have run away from them. One of the greatest Latin authors of the Middle Ages, he has left a fairly large body of writings, all of which are in a sense "occasional." He was not one who wrote because he had to. His treatises were usually composed at the request of some fellow monk, some abbot, some other churchman, to answer a question or to meet some particular need. Most of his written works are sermons. Best known, perhaps, are his letters. Finally, not least in quality though they occupy comparatively little space, come his formal treatises. Only one of these, the *De Consideratione*, exceeds the length of a long article in a serious magazine. Most of these short tracts have not been translated into English, except for the treatises, "On the Love of God," "On Conversion," and "On the Degrees of Humility." These have been not only translated but edited with notes and introductions which are not always as helpful as they seem to be. A new translation of "The Canticle of Canticles" is promised us shortly in London, and the letters have been excellently done into English, by Father Bruno James, in the edition already referred to.*

Taking a broad, general view of all Saint Bernard's writings, we find that they give us a definite and coherent doctrine, a theology, embracing not merely one department of Christian life but the whole of that life. In other words, Saint Bernard is not merely to be classified as "a spiritual writer," as if his doctrine could be limited to a certain nondogmatic region of affective intimacy with God. He is spiritual indeed, and a great mystic. But he is a speculative mystic; his mysticism is expressed as a theology. It not only describes his own personal religious experiences but it penetrates into the heart of the "Mystery of God, that is Christ" (Colossians 2:2). It contemplates and expounds the providential economy of man's redemption and sanctification. It is at once a mystical theology and a soteriology. It not only explains what it means to be united to God in Christ, but shows the meaning of the whole economy of our redemption in Christ. It tells us how to recognize the "visits" of the Word to the soul; how to respond to the action of the Holy Spirit Who is the "Law"

* See page 31.

[48]

of the inner life of God, when He comes to bring our faculties under the sway of His divine charity.

In teaching us all this, Saint Bernard does not hesitate to turn aside from contemplation in the strict sense to settle certain difficult questions of theological debate. We know that Bernard was esteemed as one of the most authoritative theologians of his time, and that his action led to the refutation of such important errors as those of Abelard and Gilbert de la Porrée.

Saint Bernard's theology of grace presupposes his Neoplatonic conception of the soul created in God's image and destined by God for a perfect union of likeness with Himself. The conception is more than Neoplatonism. The desire of the soul for God, which is in Bernard's eyes inseparable from the very freedom of the soul itself, must be elevated by grace above the level of a mere frustrated velleity. Human freedom, aided by the power of the Holy Spirit, can aspire to far more than a mere intellectual contemplation of eternal ideas: that, in Saint Bernard's mind, would be little better than frustration. God does not remain cold and distant, attracting the soul but never yielding Himself to it. He Himself both begins and finishes the work of the soul's transformation, and this whole work is an *ordinatio caritatis*, that is to say the elevation, disciplining, and redirection of all the soul's capacity for love by the actual motion of the divine Spirit. At the center of this work is Christ, in Whom and by Whom it is all effected. Bernard's devotion to the humanity of the Savior must not be regarded merely as a pious discovery intended to aid monastic meditation. It is simply a rediscovery of the Christ of the Fathers and of Saint Paul. Saint Bernard's intense love for Jesus found expression, it is true, in lyrical terms which were singularly effective in making God's mercy real to those who read his pages. But in its substance his Christology is simply the fruit of his ability "to comprehend with all the saints, what is the breadth and length and height and depth: to know also the charity of Christ which surpasseth all knowledge that you may be filled unto the fulness of God" (Ephesians 3:18-19). The basic ideas of Saint Bernard's theology are treated in the encyclical and in our commentary on it. It is sufficient here to name the Saint's chief works and to give some idea of their contents. Setting aside the letters, let us consider first his treatises and then his sermons.

"On the Degrees of Humility" (*De Gradibus Humilitatis*) is one of Saint Bernard's earliest works (1119). It summarizes the commentary of the Abbot of Clairvaux on the central doctrine of Benedictine asceticism—the seventh chapter of the rule, on monastic humility. The tract is made up of two parts, of vastly different importance. The second makes easier reading and is a lively piece of light literature that shows Bernard to be a true Frenchman and a compatriot of La Bruyère. He takes Saint Benedict's degrees of humility, turns them upside down into degrees of pride, and gives us mordant descriptions of monks on each one of the downward steps from "curiosity" to impenitent mortal sin. But the first

part of the treatise is the one that matters. It is a
formal declaration that the Cistercians, or at least
Saint Bernard, interpreted the Rule of Saint Benedict
as a preparation for the mystical life, for, says Saint
Bernard, when the monk has ascended the twelve degrees of humility, he passes through the degrees of
truth, the last of which is contemplation, or the transient experience of God in the *raptus* of divine love.
The fact that Saint Bernard talks of degrees of truth
does not mean that this is a tract on epistemology.
He is talking about a contact with truth that only
begins where epistemology leaves off: for the philosophical justification of our conceptual knowledge
of truth or of God has little to say about the experi-
ential grasp of divine things by charity which is the
subject of Bernard's *De Gradibus*.

The treatise "On the Love of God" (*De Diligendo
Deo*) again shows the unity of Saint Bernard's great
conception of man in his relations with God. The
love of God is not merely something that can somehow profitably be fitted into man's life. It is man's
whole reason for existing, and until he loves God
man does not really begin to live. Hence Saint Bernard examines the question of our universal obligation to love God, the reasons why we should love
Him ("because He is God"), and the measure of our
love ("to love Him without measure"). The four
degrees of love which are the heart of the treatise
show that it is man's very nature to love. By reason
of the fall, he who should love unselfishly now loves
himself first of all. But divine grace re-educates man's

natural love, reinstates it in its natural purity, extends it to all men, then purifies it and raises it to God. We begin by loving ourselves, pass on to the love of other men and of God for our own sakes, then begin to love God for His own sake. But the fourth degree of love is that in which we love ourselves for God's sake. This is the high point of Bernard's Christian humanism. It shows that the fulfillment of our destiny is not merely to be lost in God, as the traditional figures of speech would have it, like "a drop of water in a barrel of wine or like iron in the fire," but *found* in God in all our individual and personal reality, tasting our eternal happiness not only in the fact that we have attained to the possession of His infinite goodness, but above all in the fact that we see His will is done in us. Ultimately this perfection demands the resurrection of the bodies of all the saints, for the consummation Saint Bernard looks forward to is no mere philosophical union with the Absolute. It is the term proposed to us by Christian revelation itself: the resurrection, the general judgment, the summing up of all in Christ so that "God will be all in all." Written about the same time as the *De Diligendo Deo* (1126 or 1127), Saint Bernard's tract "On Free Will and Grace" is fundamental to his whole theology. This is one of the main sources for his doctrine on man's soul as the image of God. Liberty constitutes man in God's image. This is only another way of saying what we have already seen: man is made in order that he may love God. In order to love God with disinterested charity he must first

[52]

be free. His whole ascent to divine union is a progress in liberty. Our basic freedom, *liberum arbitrium* or freedom of choice, is only the beginning of the ascent. The capacity to choose between good and evil is only the shadow of true liberty. Genuine freedom is the work of grace. Grace finds the soul of fallen man in a state of captivity to sin. Our freedom spontaneously turns to evil rather than to good, until it is set in order by grace. Then it becomes capable of consistently avoiding evil choices. Finally by glory the soul achieves its ultimate and perfect liberty: the freedom to choose always what is good and to rejoice always in what is best, without ever being turned aside from the good by any inclination to what is less good or formally evil. We are only perfectly free in heaven, according to this doctrine of Saint Bernard.

The *Apologia*, written in 1127, is seldom translated in its entirety. But it is often quoted in part. The parts quoted are the "purple passages" in which Saint Bernard scathingly criticizes the comforts of Benedictine life at Cluny and the overwhelming splendor of the great Benedictine churches of his time. The book was written at the request of the Benedictine Abbot, William of Saint Thierry, as a reply to Peter the Venerable, Abbot of Cluny. Peter had reproved the Cistercians for taking a pharisaical attitude toward their Benedictine brethren. The *Apologia* was intended to be a defense not of Cistercian poverty but of monastic charity. Saint Bernard begins by praising the qualities of different

[53]

forms of monastic observance saying that this variety is necessary in the Church. This is not merely a diplomatic opening to a Cistercian manifesto. Bernard is not propagandizing his own Order, but defending the unity of the Church: and her unity demands variety. To compel all monks to follow the same observance would be un-Catholic. Therefore Saint Bernard devotes several pages to severe reprehension of those Cistercians who had, in fact, given the Cluniacs just cause for complaint.

There are some in our Order [he says] who are said to criticize other Orders, contrary to the words of the Apostle who said: "Do not judge before the time, until the Lord come, who both will bring to light the hidden things of darkness and will make manifest the counsels of hearts." (I Corinthians 4:5.) Desiring to set up a justice of their own they withdraw themselves from subjection to the justice of God. Such men, if such there be, I would say belonged neither to our order nor to any "order." For although they live by the rule of an order, by speaking proudly they make themselves to be citizens of Babylon, that is, of confusion. Indeed they make themselves sons of darkness, sons of hell itself wherein there is no order, but wherein everlasting horror dwells.*

If after this Bernard himself goes on to say some rather severe things about Cluniac observance, it is in the interests of the monastic order and of the Church as a whole that he does so. His just criticisms were taken to heart by the Benedictines themselves, although his austere views on art were not accepted by them. In any case he always remained on very

* *Apologia ad Gullielmum*, n. 10; P.L., 182:904.

good terms with Cluny as his correspondence with Peter the Venerable and other Benedictines can prove. The same esteem for all the different interpretations of Saint Benedict's rule can be found in the tract "On Precept and Dispensation" (*De Precepto et Dispensatione*), written in answer to several questions proposed to him by the Benedictines of Saint Peter of Chartres in 1143. This treatise is technically monastic, and is very interesting for its discussion of the value of monastic vows, the obligation to obey the Rule of Saint Benedict, obedience to monastic superiors, silence, stability, and the question of changing from one monastery to another.

Of more universal interest will be the sermon to the university students of Paris, *De Conversione*.* It is interesting that the full title of the tract reads: "Sermon Addressed to Clerics, on Conversion." What he was telling the clerics was not how to convert others but how to convert themselves. Anyone who has read the history of medieval schools and universities will recognize that Saint Bernard's remarks were probably not misplaced. The tract concerns itself first of all with the notion of the Christian conscience, on the action of divine grace in the soul through the instrumentality of the word of God, either preached or read in Scripture. Then Saint Bernard talks of the psychology of unbalanced extraversion that infallibly leads to sin, and the necessary ascetical processes of meditation, recollection, self-

* "On Conversion," translated by Watkin Williams, London, 1938.

knowledge, self-denial, which aid the work of grace. Here he is both vivid and practical, and his observations are not without a characteristic note of satire. The second part of the treatise deals with the *ordinatio caritatis*, the positive and constructive work of virtue and purification by trial which build up the interior life of the soul in Christ.

Even before this sermon, preached in 1140, Saint Bernard had written a spiritual directory for the newly formed military order of the Knights Templar. He had also had a share in the composition of their rule.

The "directory" for the Templars is called "The Praises of the New Knighthood" (*De Laude Novae Militiae*) because in the opening chapters he makes a pointed contrast between the new militia and the old "malice" (*malitia*). The only fruit of secular warfare, says Bernard, is that both the killer and the killed end in hell.* The Knight Templar who devotes his strength and his arms to the service of God can become a saint by being a good soldier. To fight in a Holy War is to become an instrument of divine justice, re-establishing the order violated by sin. Nor should the force of arms be used to restore order until all other means have failed. But in making this qualification, Bernard takes it for granted that there is no other way with the "pagans" than the way of war.

---

* "*Quis igitur finis fructusve saecularis hujus, non dico militiae sed malitiae, si et occisor letaliter peccat et occisus aeternaliter perit?*" *De Laude Novae Militiae*, n. 5; P.L., 182:923.

The third chapter of this interesting treatise shows
the basic assumptions behind Bernard's preaching of ←
the second Crusade, and they bear a striking resem-
blance to the arguments that also drove the armies
of Islam into battle. However, the directory was not
written for a crusade, but for a religious army of
occupation—men whose vocation it was to patrol
and defend the Holy Land and keep peace there.
The major part of the little book is devoted to showing the Templars how they can make their residence
in Palestine the occasion of a particularly deep life
of prayer and meditation. It does not seem that they
fully appreciated Saint Bernard's program.

Saint Bernard's tract "Against the Errors of Peter
Abelard" (1140) is important in the history of Catholic theology, most of all because in it Bernard de-
fends the strict, literal, and objective value of Christ's
redemptive death for man. For Abelard, the death of
Christ on the Cross did not, strictly speaking, redeem
man: it only offered him an example of supreme humility, charity, and self-sacrifice. Bernard asserts,
against Abelard, that Christ became man precisely
in order to redeem mankind from sin, deliver man
from the power of the devil, and to become, instead
of fallen Adam, the new head of a redeemed and
sanctified human race. Jesus, says Saint Bernard, not
only taught us justice but gave us justice. He not
only showed us His love by dying for us on the
Cross, but by the effects of His death He really and
objectively causes His charity to exist and act in our

hearts.* In doing so, He actually destroys sin in our
souls and communicates to us a new life which is
totally supernatural and divine. The effect of our
redemption is therefore a complete and literal regeneration of those souls to whom its fruits are applied.
Without this dogmatic basis the whole mystical theology of Saint Bernard would be completely incom-
prehensible. The purpose of all his mystical and
ascetic teaching is to show us how to co-operate with
the action of divine grace so that our redemption and
regeneration may not remain a dead letter but may
actually influence all our conduct and find expression
in every part of our lives until we arrive at that divine union by which the Christ-life is perfected in
our souls. It was in order to bring us to this perfect
union that Jesus died on the Cross.

Less important than the tract against Abelard is
the short treatise "On Baptism" (*De Baptismo*),
which Bernard wrote, at the request of Hugh of Saint
Victor, to answer several technical arguments that
had been raised on the subject.

Finally, not the least charming and readable of
Saint Bernard's short works is his biography of Saint
Malachy of Armagh. The saintly primate of Ireland
died at Clairvaux in 1148 and Bernard wrote his life
to console the Cistercians of Malachy's native land.
It is amusing to notice that many of the concise and
vivid expressions with which Bernard described the
qualities of his holy friend have found their way into

* *Contra Errores Abaelardi*, n. 17; P.L., 182:1067.

antiphons of Saint Bernard's own feast. The Church uses them to celebrate the virtues of the biographer himself.

We need only make a passing mention of Saint Bernard's work on Gregorian chant, which was not actually composed by him. The work was done under his guidance by a commission of abbots appointed to supervise the revision of the Cistercian choir books. He also composed a liturgical office for the martyr Saint Victor.

We have on earlier pages seen something of the *De Consideratione* (Tract on Meditation), the last and perhaps the most celebrated of Saint Bernard's formal treatises. The five books of this concise and powerful spiritual directory were composed during the last ten years of Bernard's life. He wrote the book for Pope Eugene III, and, as a modern writer has observed, in addressing Pope Eugene, Bernard was really writing for all who would ascend to the papacy. "Valuable for all prelates," says the same writer,* "and for all men, the *De Consideratione* is at the same time a valuable document on Bernard himself. . . . To all clerics, in the person of the highest among them, Bernard proposes a program inspired by the monastic tradition by which he himself lives."

The importance of the *De Consideratione* lies in its stress on the interior life and on the essential primacy of contemplation over action. The Pope must remember, says Bernard, that the interior life ought,

* Dom Jean Leclercq, O.S.B., *Saint Bernard Mystique*, pp. 197, 198.

by rights, to be preferred to exterior action.* Action
is a necessity, and we are in fact prevented from re-
maining always in silence, contemplation, study, and
prayer. But action is only valid if it is nourished by
a deep interior life. It should not absorb so much of
our time and energy that meditation, prayer, and
silent reflection become impossible.

Saint Bernard begins then by insisting on the need
for prayer above all in the life of those who have the
highest and most responsible positions in the Church.
He warns the Pope against a false zeal that might al-
low him to be carried away in the strong current of
great and important affairs. The fact that our works
are done in the service of God is not enough, by
itself, to prevent us from losing our interior life if
we let them devour all our time and all our strength.
Work is good and necessary, but too much of it
renders the soul insensitive to spiritual values, hardens
the heart against prayer and divine things. It requires
a serious effort and courageous sacrifice to resist this
hardening of heart. Therefore Saint Bernard warns
Pope Eugene against the danger that confronts him
if he lets himself be carried away by affairs of state,
and keeps no time for himself, for prayer and for the
things of God.

In giving this advice, Bernard was not thinking
only of the Pope's own soul but of the whole Church.

---

* Nam si liceret quod deceret, *absolute per omnia et in omnibus
praeferendam* . . . quae ad omnia valet, id est pietatem irrefragibilis
ratio monstrat. Quid sit pietas, quaeris? Vacare considerationi. *De
Consideratione*, Bk. I, c. vii, 8; P.L., 182:736.

His vision always extended to horizons broad enough to encompass the world and the whole Mystery of Christ. All his spiritual direction was orientated toward this Mystery. Whether he guided a pope, a bishop, a king, or a simple monk, Bernard always thought of that soul's interests in relation to its place in the Church. His direction, therefore, always centered on duties of state and on one's place in the providential plan of God. The practical advice he gives to Pope Eugene on the administration of the Roman Curia does not make this book a tract on papal policies, as is sometimes thought. Bernard soon returns to the theme of contemplation, and the whole fifth book is a profound and succinct handbook on meditation and mental prayer.

Turning to Saint Bernard's sermons, we find ourselves in fertile country. There exist about a hundred and thirty sermons of Saint Bernard preached on the various feasts of the liturgical calendar—whether the feasts of the seasons or of the saints. Then we have about a hundred and twenty more sermons, "On Diverse Subjects" (*De Diversis*), which cover practically the whole field of Bernard's theological interests and are too little studied even by monks, who would profit much from the meditation of them.

The most important of all Bernard's collections of discourses is the group of eighty-six sermons on the Canticle of Canticles (*Sermones in Cantica*), which forms his greatest and most important single work.

The commentary is incomplete. Saint Bernard died when he was about to begin explaining the third chapter, and the work was continued by an English Cistercian abbot, Gilbert of Hoyland, who was also unable to finish the work. The peculiar importance of all the sermons is in fact due to the way Saint Bernard uses them to penetrate and manifest this central fact of Christianity: the mystery of God's love revealed to men in the incarnation of His Son and in their redemption. It is the "great mystery (or sacrament) of Godliness" (*magnum pietatis sacramentum*) that occupies him before all else. What is that mystery? Not an idea, not a doctrine, but a Person: God Himself, revealed in the Man, Christ. How is this doctrine understood? When the Person is known. How is He known? When loved. How loved? When He lives in us and is Himself our love for His Father. Loving the Father in us, He makes us one with the Father as He Himself is. Therefore Saint Bernard can logically say, "Truly I must love Him perfectly, in whom I have my being, my life and my knowledge. . . . Clearly, Lord Jesus, that man is worthy of death who refuses to live for thee: indeed he is already dead. And he who does not know thee by love [*sapit*] knows nothing. And he who cares to be for anything else but thee, is destined for nothingness, and is become nothing." *

I think it would be well to define the whole issue Saint Bernard's sermons raise, by two quotations

* *In Cantica*, Sermon 20, n. 1; P.L., 183:867.

from Gerard Manley Hopkins which will help the modern reader to understand something of what Saint Bernard meant by the mystery of Christ. First, writing to Robert Bridges, the poet remarks on the meaning of the mystery of Christ to a non-Catholic and to a Catholic. To a non-Catholic, the mystery of Christ is a puzzle. To a Catholic it is a Person.

To you [says Hopkins to Bridges] it comes to: Christ is in some sense God and in some sense He is not God—and your interest is in the uncertainty; to the Catholic it is: Christ is in every sense God and in every sense man, and the interest is in the locked and inseparable combination, or rather it is in the *Person* in whom the combination has its place.

These were exactly Saint Bernard's sentiments toward Abelard's treatment of the dogma of redemption.*

The second quotation from Hopkins illustrates Saint Bernard's idea that we fulfill the end for which we were created when, by conformity to Christ, we fully realize our own identity by becoming perfectly free and therefore by loving God without limit. Hopkins says: "This [conformity to Christ] brings out the nature of the man himself as the lettering on a sail or the device upon a flag are best seen when it fills."

All Saint Bernard's sermons more or less fit into the scope defined by these two statements. The scope is, of course, practically limitless. But these are his two great themes: the mystery of Christ in Himself

* *Contra Errores Abaelardi*, n. 17; P.L., 182:1067.

and in those who are conformed to Him in the Holy Spirit. In other words: Christ and the Church.

The finest and most characteristic pages of Saint Bernard on this doctrine are probably to be found in his Advent and Christmas sermons, his sermons on the Virgin Mother (*Homiliae super Missus Est*) and on some of her great feasts, as well as in some of the more important sermons on the Canticle.

Advent and Christmas seem to have exercised a more powerful attraction over Saint Bernard and the early Cistercians than any other phases of the liturgical cycle. Here the emphasis is on the Incarnation—on the redemption as it is seen from the viewpoint of the Incarnation rather than from that of the Passion. The "Sacrament of Advent," as Saint Bernard calls it, is the mystery of Christ's presence in the world. It is an important concept, for the Incarnation is not a mere matter of history but a present reality, and the most important reality of all. For it is the one reality that gives significance to everything else that has ever happened. Without it, nothing in history has any ultimate meaning.

If Christ is present, if His Kingdom is "in the midst of us," it is because of the infinite mercy of God. Only a divine decree could decide His coming, His descent into the darkness of a world which, without Him, would be doomed to everlasting despair. Bernard, in his characteristic emphasis on freedom and charity, sees this mystery of divine mercy above all as a supremely free and gratuitous act of God: but it is not a purely arbitrary act, since it depends on the "law" of goodness which rules all God's acts.

In the contemplation of this mystery, Bernard is never abstract. He is always talking about the great concrete facts revealed to us in the Bible, and his sermons are alive with images and figures out of the Scriptures. Color, music, movement, fire, contrasts of light and darkness, impassioned dialogue between the poverty of man and the greatness of God, between the mercy of God and His justice, flights of allegory, realistic examples sketched from life in the cloister—all these elements make Bernard's sermons extraordinarily alive. Indeed the very wealth of them sometimes oppresses the reader who has lost his sense of symbolism, or never had one. All the opulence that Bernard criticized in the plastic arts here runs riot in his prose, but without the exaggeration, the caricature, the grotesque, the crudeness that he reproved. At the heart of all this is the beautiful simplicity of his doctrine itself, in which there is nothing difficult, nothing esoteric, nothing complicated: only the depth and the lucidity of the Gospel. "It does not behoove thee, O man," says the Saint, "to cross the seas, to penetrate the clouds, or to climb the Alps [in search of God]. No great journey is necessary for thee. Seek no further than thy own soul: there wilt thou find thy God!" *Usque ad temetipsum occurre Deo tuo.* *

The practical details of the interior life and of this

---

* Sermon 1, Advent, nn. 10-11.

search for God are elaborated with greater finesse in a series like the Lenten sermons on Psalm Ninety, preached to the monks of Clairvaux in the year 1139. But the greatest richness and variety of all are found in the sermons on the Canticle. Saint Bernard was more than explaining the text of this Song of Songs. He lived it, and blended the traditional mystical interpretation of the Canticle with the experience of his own union with God. As we see in *Doctor Mellifluus*, it is in these sermons that Saint Bernard's mystical doctrine reaches its most perfect elaboration. But there is also much in them besides mysticism. There is the lament for the death of his brother, Gerard (Sermon 26). There are attacks on the Manichaean heresy (Sermons 64-66) and on the trinitarian errors of Gilbert de la Porrée (Sermon 80). There are remarks on monastic observance, on the chanting of the divine office in choir, on the relations of the active and contemplative lives, as well as on all the Christian virtues.

Above all, the sermons on the Canticle are a magnificent treatise on the union of Christ and His Church. The mystical union of the Word with the individual soul is simply an expression of the union of the Incarnate Word with His Church. And this, as the encyclical demonstrates, brings us to the real inner unity that binds everything together in the life and work of Bernard of Clairvaux. In all that he writes, in all that he says, in all that he does, Bernard has only one end in view: the integration of nations, dioceses, monasteries, and individuals into the life and order of the Church.

Bernard is a builder, a man at once of liberty and of order, a man who builds individual liberties into a universal order, that all may be more perfectly free. In other words, Bernard is a man of the Church, *Vir Ecclesiae*. This fact, and this alone, explains the miraculous resources which enabled him to become the greatest man of his time.

3

NOTES ON THE ENCYCLICAL
DOCTOR MELLIFLUUS

S ITS TITLE indicates, *Doctor Mellifluus* discusses Saint Bernard as a Father and Doctor of the Church. That is to say it reminds us that the doctrine of Saint Bernard is one of the purest and most authentic sources of Catholic tradition. The encyclical summarizes the great truths which the Church herself teaches us through Bernard of Clairvaux. The Fathers of the Church speak to us as "organs of the Holy Spirit." They teach with a supernaturally enlightened genius, "not in the learned words of human wisdom, but in the doctrine of the Spirit, comparing spiritual things with spiritual" (I Corinthians 2:13). Their doctrine penetrates the "deep things of God" and scrutinizes the mysteries of faith not merely with the light of human dialectics, but with the far more searching light of charity which knows God less by "seeing" than by "tasting" the very substance of His goodness. The doctrine of the Fathers is something more than a science. It is *wisdom*, which rises to a knowledge of God and of the things of God in the infinite riches of the love of Christ. Therefore, unlike the dialectical science which leads from abstract principles to a grasp of truth in an abstract and universal formulation, the wisdom of the Fathers embraces the truth in its concreteness, in its reality. It knows God not as the "First

[71]

Mover," the "Supreme Being," or as a Creator contained in a formula or article of faith: it goes beyond the words we believe in and attains to Him Whom we believe. Theological science is the dialectical effort of "faith in search of understanding," but theological wisdom is the repose of the soul in an embrace of love that attains to God beyond all understanding. And yet this wisdom, taught by the angels, has the audacity to seek to express itself in human language. Bernard of Clairvaux was one of its most humble and audacious disciples.

"Wisdom" is not the exclusive prerogative of the Fathers. It overflowed from the ardent preaching of the Apostles. It was the goal of the great scholastic theologians, like Saint Thomas Aquinas and Saint Bonaventure. It burst forth in the living flame of love that transformed the souls of Saint John of the Cross and Saint Teresa. All the great doctors and contemplatives were sanctified by the spirit of wisdom. But, as the proper Mass of Saint Bernard, in the Cistercian missal, informs us, wisdom played a very special role in the vocation of Saint Bernard. The liturgy suggests that he was wedded to divine wisdom as Saint Francis was wedded to Lady Poverty. The text of the Gradual applies to Saint Bernard these words from the Book of Wisdom: "I have loved wisdom, and have sought her out from my youth, and have desired to take her for my spouse, and have loved her for her beauty" (Wisdom 8:2).

Saint Bernard, writing just before the age of the

great scholastics, brought to a grand conclusion the tradition of the Fathers. The theologians of the thirteenth century would construct a great dialectical edifice from earth to heaven, by uniting truths of faith with the principles of Aristotelian philosophy. Saint Bernard belonged to the line of those who, instead of ascending from earth to heaven, came down from heaven to earth descending like Moses from the cloud on Sinai, his face transfigured with divine light, and promulgating the "immaculate Law of God, which is Charity." *

"Cistercian mysticism," says Etienne Gilson, "is altogether suspended from a theology of the Trinity of which the central idea would seem to be that God Himself lives by a law, and that *the law that rules His intimate life is love.* The Father generates the Son, and the bond that unites the Son to the Father and the Father to the Son is the Spirit Who is their mutual love. . . . It is as if this law of love, participated in by things, were the eternal law, the creative and directive law of the universe, but more particularly of man in whom it reigns as charity." † In other words, God is love. And because God "has first loved us" (I John 4:19) we are able to become His sons. Made in the image of God, we become perfectly like Him by becoming like His Son, Jesus. This likeness is a participation in the charity, the bond or "law" of love which is the unity of the Father and the Son:

* "*Lex Domini immaculata caritas est,*" Saint Bernard, *De Diligendo Deo,* n. 35; P.L., 182:996.
† Etienne Gilson, *The Spirit of Medieval Philosophy,* p. 298.

that is to say, the Holy Spirit. Perfect charity makes us able to "see" God.

This concept of a charity which starts in God and reaches down to elevate the creature and deify him by union with the Word distinguished the wisdom of Saint Bernard from that of the scholastics. Wisdom, according to Saint Bonaventure, is indeed a divine likeness. But it is *impressed on the soul by our desire for God.** Love, the likeness to God which makes us wise as He is wise, is more than a desire for God in the doctrine of Saint Bernard. The wisdom of love is *impressed upon our soul by God's desire for us.*†

Now the principal theme of *Doctor Mellifluus* is Saint Bernard's teaching on charity and on the elevation of the soul to divine union by the mercy of Him who has "first loved us."

No one has ever doubted that Saint Bernard deserved to be numbered among the Fathers of the Church to the extent that he thought and wrote as they did. But if some have hesitated in the past to accord him that title, on the grounds that he lived in the twelfth century and did not enjoy sufficient "antiquity," this encyclical does much to dispel their hesitations. The opening sentence of *Doctor Mel-*

---

* "*Per deiformitatem sapientia imprimitur, quia desiderando deiformitate ad sapientiam venimus,*" Saint Bonaventure, *Collatio ii in Hexaemeron.*

† Such is the thought of a modern Cistercian writer on Saint Bernard. Père Maurice Dumontier contrasts the scholastic formula, "*Deus movet sicut desideratum,*" with what might have been a comparable formula summing up the doctrine of Saint Bernard: "*Deus movet sicut desiderans.*" See P. Dumontier, *Saint Bernard et la Bible,* Paris, 1953, p. 39.

Notes on the Encyclical

lifluus concedes the title of Father of the Church to Bernard of Clairvaux, by quoting the famous words of Mabillon: "The Mellifluous Doctor, the last of the Fathers, but certainly not unequal to the earlier ones."

After a brief preamble which declares that Saint Bernard's supereminence in the history of his time was due to his sanctity and wisdom, and after recalling the praises which have been heaped on the Abbot of Clairvaux by popes, historians, and non-Catholics,* the Holy Father introduces us at once to his doctrine. He does so not only for the benefit of the members of the Saint's own contemplative Order—the Cistercians of the various Observances—but for all who take delight in what is true, beautiful, and holy.

The source of Bernard's wisdom, says the encyclical, was the continual meditation of Scripture and the Fathers. The Holy Father then proceeds to distinguish the wisdom of Saint Bernard from true and false philosophy, reminding us that the only philosophy Saint Bernard despised was the false "curiosity" which could not lead to the true knowledge of God because it blinded us to our need for His merciful love.

Opposed to this curiosity, the science that "puffeth up" because it is without charity, is the true theology which Bernard loved with the most ardent devotion. This theology, as the Holy Father points out in three succinct quotations from Saint Bernard, is a wisdom rather than a science. It is not only a perception of

* Calvin said of Saint Bernard, "The Abbot Bernard speaks in the language of the truth itself," and Luther said, "Bernard surpasses all the other Doctors of the Church."

the divine truth by understanding but an embrace of
that truth by love. Both these elements of knowledge
and love are absolutely essential for true wisdom, for
"What would be the good of learning without love?
It would puff us up. And love without learning? It
would go astray." This is one of those many instances
in which Saint Bernard's Latin loses all its character in
translation. The original must be seen to be fully appreciated: *"Quid faceret eruditio absque dilectione?
Inflaret. Quid absque eruditione dilectio? Erraret."* *

Saint Bernard, the Doctor of Mystical Love, must
necessarily be a defender of truth and of learning. God
Himself is wisdom. Therefore He can only be loved
fittingly if He is loved wisely. Neglect of knowledge
leads love into error, and the enemy of souls has no
more efficacious way of drawing God's love out of
our hearts, Saint Bernard says, than by inducing us to
seek Him without the light of intelligence.

Summarizing these texts from the Saint, Pope Pius
XII concludes that the whole purpose of Saint Bernard's study and contemplation was to rise above
human subtleties and, uniting the rays of truth in one
shaft of loving contemplation, to direct them all together upon the highest truth. "This," says the Holy
Father, "is indeed true wisdom, which transcends all
human things and draws back all things to their
source, which is God, in order to convert men to
Him." Soaring above the dialecticians of his time, Bernard flew like an eagle to the highest peak of truth.

---

* *In Cantica,* Sermon 69, n. 2; P.L., 183:1113.

Doctrine was not, for him, an end, only a means. To what? To mystical union. And the Holy Father sanctions something of the bold language of mysticism when he adds that in this union with God the soul of Bernard "from time to time enjoyed something not far short of infinite happiness, even though still in this life."

After a paragraph in which he praises the vivid and eloquent Latin style of Saint Bernard and declares that the Holy Spirit sheds an inextinguishable light over those pages, many of which have found a place in the liturgy, Pope Pius XII returns to the main theme: mystical wisdom. It is hard to imagine how his treatment of the theme could have been more direct, more forceful, or more succinct.

The Holy Father not only plunges directly into the texts which give us the deepest and most definitive expression of Saint Bernard's mystical doctrine but in doing so he remarks explicitly that these texts will be for the "utility of all." Far from a vague and general commendation of Saint Bernard's teaching, we find ourselves confronted with the clearest and most fundamental statements of the Mellifluous Doctor on the mystical marriage of the soul with God. They are all taken from the eighty-third sermon on the Canticle of Canticles, written shortly before Saint Bernard's death, and representing the highest development of his thought.

Now the opening lines of this sermon, which Pope Pius quotes extensively, declare that every soul, no matter how burdened with sins, no matter how conscious of its exile from God, and no matter how close it may be to damnation and to despair, can nevertheless find in itself a reason to hope not only for pardon, not only for mercy, but even for perfect union with God in "the mystical marriage." The context of these lines shows that Saint Bernard was here developing his doctrine of the soul as image of God, created for the most perfect union with Him. The same sermon goes on, as we shall see, to discuss the characteristics of this perfect mystical union. However, Saint Bernard's statement, as it stands, really contributes little to the speculative question of a "universal call to mystical prayer." It is far beyond speculation and dialectics. It is a tremendous insight into the bottomless abyss of the divine mercy, and its value is much more practical, much more immediate and much more precious than if it merely provided the controversialist with another shaft for his quiver.

It would be hard to say, with certainty, whether Saint Bernard thought that the vocation to sanctity also implied a vocation to mystical prayer. Supremely unconcerned with the problems that agitate modern theologians on this point, Bernard had his eyes fixed on the end of our journey in heaven, and on the perfect union of the risen Church with God in the glory that is to come after the resurrection of all flesh. Mystical union and rapture in this life are treated by him as transient foretastes of this glory. They are things which he encourages his monks to pray for and which, according to the words we have just quoted, any

Christian may desire. He does not explain what chance each one may have of arriving at them in this life. For Saint Bernard did not stop to consider even mystical union as an end in itself.

Pope Pius clarifies this passage of Saint Bernard when he interprets it to mean that all men can and must aspire to perfect sanctity in the sense of an active union of wills with God by renunciation and fervent charity: ". . . All can and must from time to time lift their hearts from the earthly things around them to those of heaven, and most earnestly love the Supreme Dispenser of all gifts." As for graces of infused or mystical prayer, the Holy Father reminds us that it is not actually possible for all to experience them at will. The highest mystical graces, and even the lowest, for that matter, are pure gifts of God. We are all permitted to desire them. To gain them, however, it is not sufficient to ask for them or to desire them. There is no way in which they can, strictly speaking, be earned. God grants these gifts to whom He wills, and one who has not received them does not have to feel guilty on that account. The mercy of God is by no means confined to a few consolations of prayer in this life. These are only crumbs fallen from the table of the heavenly banquet. It remains for each one of us to do what is actually possible with the help of ordinary grace: to love God with all the strength of his will. And this is nothing but the first commandment. Bernard himself has left us his own clear teaching on this point.

It is not given to all [he says] to enjoy the glad and secret presence of the Spouse in the same way, but only in the way destined for each one by the Spouse's Father. It is not we who choose Him, He chooses us; and wherever each one of us is placed by Him: that is where he stands.*

In making this interpretation of Saint Bernard's doctrine the Holy Father does not actually touch on the speculative questions which have been raised in our time. He does not say whether or not mystical graces are to be considered part of the normal development of the life of sanctifying grace. He does not exclude a remote general call to mystical prayer. He simply says that in practice few souls can expect to reach the highest degree of mystical union in this present life. Everyone knows that very few actually do so. Theologians commonly agree that there is no harm in anyone desiring to do so, provided he desires it with humility. In any case, we might remark that the way to perfect union with God is not a way of exaltation: for "everyone that exalteth himself shall be humbled." That is why the naïve enthusiasm of those who plunge with rash ambition into the ways of prayer so often ends in nervous breakdown. The worst possible way to become a saint is to aspire to a sanctity in which one can admire oneself and be admired by others: for self-complacency is the very opposite of sanctity. False contemplation can be attained by the prudence of the flesh, but true mysticism is a gift that is granted only to those who are extremely little and poor in their own eyes, and who

* *In Cantica,* Sermon 23, n. 9; P.L., 183:809.

have learned, as Bernard himself did, to live not for
themselves but for others. Such things are only learned
supernaturally from the Holy Spirit.

Returning to Pope Pius's discussion of Bernard's
mysticism, we find a succinct outline of Saint Bernard's eighty-third sermon on the Canticle. It is
summed up in long quotations, and here is their content.

First, as we have seen, every man should aspire to
perfect union with God, at least in heaven. The fact
that we are made in God's image should lead us to do
this without any fear. The perfection of love, indeed,
demands that we cast out all fear and seek the mercy
of God with perfect confidence.

Secondly, this union is a "marriage" with the Word
of God. It is a union of wills in which the soul becomes "equal" to Him by loving Him as it is loved
by Him. Identity in perfect union of wills, oneness
in charity makes us "one Spirit" with God, so that
we live by His life and love with His love rather than
with our own. This union is full of all joy, because it
means that the soul is constantly moved and guided
by God Himself, is never separated from the Word,
and is enlightened and directed by His Spirit in all
things, no limit being placed on the sharing of love
except the limit set by its own desires. Bernard makes
clear that this is more than a moral union, more than
a kind of agreement or contract: it is a mystical union
or an embrace of beings fused into one without, however, losing their own proper identities. Once this
union is achieved the soul has nothing to live for but

[81]

pure and selfless love and this love is God Himself. *"Qui amat, amat et aliud novit nihil!"* *

Thirdly, since God Himself is love, nothing can give Him greater honor than our love. Consequently nothing could be more meritorious than this pure love by which we abandon all and live for God alone. What does love merit? More love. For charity is at once the merit and the reward. *Ipse praemium, ipse meritum est sibi.* But why? Because, though there must always be a distinction between the uncreated Love Who is God Himself and the created love by which He gives us participation in Himself, nevertheless our charity plunges always into the inexhaustible abyss of His charity in order to give back to Him what it has received from Him. Hence love alone makes the creature equal to its God, and therefore capable of perfect union with Him.

Turning to our own world, the Holy Father laments the fact this charity has grown cold. The love of God is not known. The doctrine of this divine union has been forgotten by those who lose themselves in the cares and business of increasingly active lives. They have forgotten the meaning of contemplation and of that charity which is fed not by human enthusiasm and the inspirations of natural ambition but by God Himself in prayer and sacrifice.

Pope Pius insists that we turn again to the pages of Saint Bernard in order to meditate on his doctrine of mystical love and union with God: "Since love for

---

* "He who loves, loves and that is all he knows." *In Cantica*, Sermon 83, n. 3; P.L., 183:1182.

God is gradually growing cold today in the hearts of many, or is even not infrequently completely quenched, we feel that these writings of the Mellifluous Doctor should be attentively meditated." This is necessary, he says, if we are to recover something of the true fervor of Christian living not only in our private lives but also in society as a whole. What hope can there be of men living at peace together when they do not love one another? And how can they love one another as brothers if they do not love God, their common Father? If we have no feeling for the reality of God's love for us, we cannot respect the duties of fraternal charity or even of strict justice which we owe to the men we live with. It is therefore necessary that the kind of charity about which Saint Bernard wrote should be once more enkindled in the hearts of all Catholics if we are to see a revival of true Christianity in the world.

The Holy Father goes on to point out that this obligation to meditate on Saint Bernard and to imitate his life of contemplation and love for God binds especially those who have made vows in the monastic Order of which he is the glory. Cistercians, in their hidden monasteries, must not only read Saint Bernard and talk about him and write about him: they must keep alive in the world the charity which he has left them as their special inheritance. It is far more essential to their vocation than anything else, whether it be liturgy, or austerity, or material expansion, or preached retreats, or fidelity to the externals of monastic tradition. With charity, with love for God and his brothers, the Cistercian is a true monk. Without them, no matter how well he may do any other thing, he is not a monk. He might as well return to the world. Clerics also and especially priests are urged by the Holy Father to make this doctrine their own and live it out in their ministry. In every sphere of civil and religious life, and especially in Christian homes, the encyclical would welcome a revival of this perfect charity. Saint Bernard's doctrine, after all, flows directly from the Gospels, and that is why it is so important in our time of revolution and of war. Inspired by divine charity, men can practice any other virtue with ease. Without charity there is no hope of peace, of happiness or of any other true good: for all these goods come from God alone. But they cannot come to those who are not united to Him by love.

"No one," says the Holy Father, "has ever spoken of divine charity so magnificently, so profoundly, so powerfully as Saint Bernard." And in a few brief quotations the Holy Father shows that this doctrine of love is a doctrine of self-sacrifice. The more Saint Bernard came to know of God in the silence and solitude of his contemplative prayer, the more he felt that the "sleep" of contemplation was in reality an awakening to a higher life, a life of more perfect and more fruitful action and a rich source of apostolic charity. Contemplation had taught Bernard not to live for himself, not to rest in the lazy inactivity of a comfortable cell, but that "each one is bound to live not for himself but for all." * This contemplative charity explains Bernard's most ardent devotion to the Church and to the Holy See. He was a "man of the Church" precisely because he was a man of God, and his great graces of prayer had been given him not for himself but for the whole Church.

The incredible labors of Saint Bernard are cited in this part of the encyclical, and the Holy Father asks by what power a monk without human support and without earthly resources could overcome such gigantic obstacles. The strength of Bernard lay in his humility, and his humility, which made it impossible for him to place any confidence in his own weakness, drove him in turn to an unlimited confidence in our Divine Redeemer and His most Blessed Mother.

It was humility that led Saint Bernard into the cloister, to seek truth and to fly from the false values of a world dominated by ambition. Humility was therefore the foundation upon which the Holy Spirit raised the fabulous structure of Saint Bernard's apostolic career. Only a heroic humility could justify the unabashed sincerity with which Saint Bernard warned and advised the great men of his time. In order to be heroic, humility must be nourished not only by the view of our own nothingness, but above all by a true sense of the greatness and the goodness of God. Saint Bernard, then, as the Holy Father tells us, was humble because he was above all a contemplative.

The sanctity of the saints is nothing but an aspect

* *"Nec cuiquam sibi sed omnibus esse vivendum." In Cantica,* Sermon 41, n. 6; P.L., 183:987.

of the sanctity of Jesus Christ. The virtues of our Holy Redeemer become our own through the marriage of our wills with His grace. If we are to be strong, Saint Bernard says, He must be strong in us. He must be our love. He must be our humility. He must be our joy. Pope Pius XII quotes the famous passage on the Holy Name, which shows what power Saint Bernard drew from the fact that Jesus was always on his lips and in his heart.

Finally, the climax of the encyclical is a long and beautiful quotation on the Blessed Virgin Mary. It reminds us that Saint Bernard is one of the greatest and most important theologians of Mary in the Catholic Church. Pope Pius XII's proclamation of 1954 as a "Marian year" invites us to dwell for a moment on Saint Bernard's Mariology.

A modern theologian writes of Bernard, saying: "It is impossible to speak or write adequately of Mary without having first studied what Saint Bernard has written about her." * Dante, in the sublime final cantos of his *Paradiso*, has exalted Saint Bernard as the greatest contemplative saint, and has, at the same time, shown how Bernard's love for Our Lady had made the whole Church more capable of contemplating and understanding the Mystery of Divine Mercy which was accomplished in her. Saint Bernard stands at a critical point in the development of theological teaching on the Mother of God. Before him it can be said that there was, strictly speaking, no such thing as a completely developed "Mariology." The prin-

* G. Roschini, O.S.M., *Il Dottore Mariano*, Rome, 1953, p. vii.

ciples were there. The seeds had long lain hidden in
the fertile soil of tradition. They had pierced the
surface of the ground in the early Fathers and in such
great ecumenical councils as that of Ephesus. But in
Bernard they first reach maturity and become ready
for the harvest. His Marian doctrine is a luminous
synthesis of all that tradition had indicated before his
time, and the loving explication of deep truths which
had hitherto lain hidden implicitly in the Mystery of
the Incarnation itself. I have already said that Bernard's writings on Mary are the most beautiful pages
he ever composed. However, they are more than
poetry, more than beautiful style; they are great
theology. To say that Saint Bernard has developed a
strict Mariology is to say that he has drawn from
Scripture not only food for affective piety, but also
principles of a new theological synthesis. The mar-
row of his teaching is concentrated in the Homilies
on the *Missus Est* (the Gospel text of the Annunciation) and seven great sermons for feasts of Our Lady,
especially the sermon on her nativity which Pope Pius
XII quotes in his encyclical.

The fundamental principle on which Saint Bernard builds his whole structure is the dogma that since
Jesus Christ is the Incarnate Word of God, and since
He entered into this world as man only by being
born of the Blessed Virgin Mary, it follows that
Mary is the Mother of God. What is more, this divine
motherhood was, in fact, dependent on her own free
choice. It was freely and knowingly that, in the sublime mystical experience of the Annunciation, she

consented to this divine motherhood. Her consent therefore gives her an altogether unique and central place in the economy of our redemption. These two facts show clearly that Mary's vocation and mission in the world are of an altogether unique and singular character. She is much closer to her Son than she is to other men. Although she too is among the redeemed, she has an utterly unique place by the side of the Redeemer—a place which no one else could ever claim. This place speaks of her supereminent sanctity, a sanctity worthy of being matched with the divine sanctity of her Son. Her mission as Mother of God therefore implies privileges and graces and dignities which could have been granted to no other human being. And they give Mary a place in the spiritual life of every Christian. If she is the Mother of the historical Christ, she is also the Mother of the Mystical Christ. The coming of the Redeemer depended on her consent, and therefore our redemption also depended on her consent. The love of Christ necessarily also implies love for His Virgin Mother. Gratitude to Him implies gratitude to her. Dependence on Him also brings with it, in a different but no less real sense, dependence on her. He is always the One Mediator, the One Redeemer. She adds nothing to the essence of His mediation, His redeeming act. But her love for us, her mediation, her co-redemptive action are included and absorbed, as it were, in His unique mediation. Better than anyone else, Saint Bernard saw that the love of Jesus and Mary are so inseparable as to be the same. We cannot love Him without at the same time loving her, and our only reason for loving her is that we may love Him better. The logical consequence of this is Saint Bernard's belief that everything that comes to us through our One Divine Mediator comes to us also, and by that very fact, through Mary. *"Totum nos habere voluit per Mariam."* *

Two succinct quotations by Pope Pius on this doctrine seem to foreshadow a dogmatic definition of Our Lady's universal mediation. Nothing could be more fitting than that this great encyclical on Saint Bernard should be, as it were, the morning star, anticipating the rising of yet another prerogative of Our Lady into the full light of faith. Saint Bernard himself could wish for no greater honor, in his centenary, than that of being recognized as the Doctor who most clearly and most forcefully bore witness to a truth so dear to the Church.

Pope Pius XII concludes by exhorting all Christians to imitate Saint Bernard's faith in Our Lady. The peace of the world is in her hands. She is the one who teaches us to love God perfectly, not merely by word or by example but by her powerful mediation which, as it were, forms Christ in our souls. Saint Bernard is there to remind us that our spiritual life springs up from her Immaculate Heart.

Doctor Mellifluus is not a long encyclical. The illness of the Holy Father in the first months of 1953 doubtless prevented all thought of a lengthier treat-

* "He willed us to have all through Mary." *Sermon in Nativitate B.V.M.*, n. 7; P.L., 183:441.

ment. But there was no need of anything longer. Vital, rich, and concise, full of clear and powerful statements drawn from the pages of Saint Bernard himself, this document gains in power by its brevity. Rarely, if ever, has such unqualified praise been given, in a papal encyclical, to the person and the doctrine of one of the saints.

What could be clearer than its great message? It is a call to sanctity, to divine union, uttered in our own troubled time by the Vicar of Jesus Christ with all the impassioned ardor of the great Saint Bernard himself. We are called to be saints, not by our own power because we have no power: but by the power of Christ's grace, and "lest the Cross of Christ be made void" (I Corinthians 1:17). We are called not merely to fear God or to honor Him, but to love Him with all our strength, love Him to the point of utter self-forgetfulness and identification with Him. And why all this? There can be no other reason than this: God is charity, and charity alone gives Him the highest glory.

ENCYCLICAL LETTER
OF HIS HOLINESS
POPE PIUS XII
on the occasion of
THE EIGHTH CENTENARY
OF THE DEATH
OF SAINT BERNARD

PIUS PP XII

VENERABLE BRETHREN

HEALTH AND APOSTOLIC BENEDICTION

THE MELLIFLUOUS DOCTOR, "the last of the Fathers, but certainly not unequal to the earlier ones," [1] was remarkable for such qualities of nature and of mind, which were enriched by God with heavenly gifts, that amid the varied and oftentimes stormy events of his age, he seemed to dominate by his sanctity, wisdom, and most prudent counsel. Wherefore, he has been lauded with great praise not only by the Sovereign Pontiffs and writers of the Catholic Church, but also and not infrequently by nonbelievers. Thus when, in the midst of universal jubilation, our predecessor Alexander III, of happy memory, inscribed him among the canonized saints, he wrote reverently: "We have passed in review the holy and venerable life of this same blessed man, showing how, with the assistance of a special gift of grace, he was not only in himself a shining example of sanctity and religion, but also radiated brilliance throughout the entire Church of God through faith and doctrine. There is hardly a

[1] Mabillon, *Bernardi Opera*, *Praef. generalis*, n. 23; Migne, P.L., 182:26.

corner of holy Christendom which does not know of the fruit he produced in the house of God by word and example; since he transmitted the precepts of our holy religion even to foreign and barbarian nations, and called back a countless multitude of sinners . . . to the right path of the spiritual life." [2] "He was," as Cardinal Baronius writes, "a truly apostolic man, even a genuine apostle sent by God, mighty in work and word, everywhere and in all things adding luster to his apostolate through the signs that followed, so that he was in nothing inferior to the great apostles . . . and should be called . . . at one and the same time an adornment and a bulwark of the entire Catholic Church." [3]

To these encomiums of highest praise, to which almost countless others could be added, we turn our thoughts at the end of this eighth century since the restorer and promoter of the Holy Cistercian Order piously departed from this mortal life, which he had adorned with such great brilliance of doctrine and splendor of sanctity. It is a source of gratification so to meditate on his merits and to set them forth in writing that, not only the members of his own Order, but also all those who find their delights principally in whatever is true, beautiful, or holy, may feel themselves spurred on to imitate the brilliant example of his virtues.

His doctrine was drawn almost exclusively from

[2] Litt. Apost., *Contigit olim*, 15 Kal. Feb., 1174, Anagniae d.
[3] *Annal.*, t. 12, *An.* 1153, p. 385, D-E, Rome, *ex Tipografia Vaticana*, 1907.

the pages of Sacred Scripture and from the Holy Fathers, which he had at hand day and night in his profound meditations; and not from the subtle reasonings of dialecticians and philosophers, which on more than one occasion he appeared to hold in low esteem.⁴ But it should be remarked that he does not reject that human philosophy which is genuine philosophy, namely, that which leads to God, to correct living, and to Christian wisdom. Rather does he repudiate that philosophy which, by recourse to empty verbiage and sophistry, aspires with presumptuous boldness to ascend to divine heights and to delve into all the secrets of God, with the result that, as often happened in those days, it violated the integrity of faith and fell miserably into heresy.

"Do you see . . ," he wrote, "how [Saint Paul the Apostle ⁵] makes the fruit and the utility of knowledge consist in the way we know? What is meant by 'the way we know'? Is it not only this, that you should recognize in what order, with what application, for what purpose and what things you should know? In what order—that you may first learn what is more conducive to salvation; with what zeal—that you may learn the more ardently what incites you the more earnestly to love; for what purpose—that you may not learn for vain glory, curiosity, or anything of the kind, but only for your own edification and that of your neighbor. For there are some who

⁴ Cf. Sermon in *Festo SS. Apost. Petri et Pauli*, n. 3; P.L., 183:407, and Sermon 3 in *Festo Pentec.*, n. 5; P.L., 183:332-B.
⁵ Cf. I Corinthians 8:2.

want knowledge for the sole purpose of knowing, and this is unseemly curiosity. And there are some who seek knowledge in order to be known themselves; and this is unseemly vanity . . . and there are also those who seek knowledge in order to sell their knowledge, for example, for money or for honors; and this is unseemly quest for gain. But there are also those who seek knowledge in order to edify and this is charity. And there are those who seek knowledge in order to be edified, and this is prudence." [6]

In the following words, he describes most appropriately the doctrine, or rather the wisdom, which he follows and ardently loves: "It is the spirit of wisdom and understanding which, like a bee bearing both wax and honey, is able both to kindle the light of knowledge and to pour in the savor of grace. Hence, let neither one think he has received the "kiss" [*i.e.,* of mystical grace], neither he who understands the truth but does not love it, nor he who loves the truth but does not understand it." [7] "What would be the good of learning without love? It would puff us up. And love without learning? It would go astray." [8] "Merely to shine is futile; merely to burn is not enough; to burn and to shine is perfect." [9] Then he explains the source of true and genuine doctrine, and how it must be united with charity: "God is Wisdom,

[6] *In Cantica,* Sermon 36, n. 3; P.L., 183:968-c, d.
[7] *Ibid.,* Sermon 8, n. 6; P.L., 183:813-a, b.
[8] *Ibid.,* Sermon 69, n. 2; P.L., 183:1113-a.
[9] *In Nat. S. Joan. Bapt.,* Sermon 3; P.L., 183:399-b.

and wants to be loved not only affectionately, but also wisely. . . . Otherwise, if you neglect knowledge, the spirit of error will most easily lay snares for your zeal; nor has the cunning enemy a more efficacious means of removing love from the heart, than if he can make a man walk carelessly and imprudently in the path of love." [10]

From these words it is clear that in his study and his contemplation under the influence of love rather than through the subtlety of human reasoning, Bernard's sole aim was to direct toward the Supreme Truth all the rays of truth which he had assembled from many different sources; drawing from them light for the mind, the fire of charity for the soul, and correct norms for the guidance of conduct. This is indeed true wisdom, which transcends all things human, and brings everything back to its source, that is, to God, in order to convert men to Him. The Mellifluous Doctor makes his way with deliberate care through the uncertain and precarious circuits of reasoning, not trusting in the keenness of his own mind nor depending upon the labored and artful syllogisms which many of the dialecticians of his time frequently abused, but, like an eagle, attempting to fix his eyes on the sun, he pushes on with swift flight to the summit of truth.

The charity which activated him makes light of obstacles and, so to speak, gives wings to the mind. For him, learning is not the final goal, but rather a path leading to God; it is not the cold object of empty

10 *In Cantica,* Sermon 19, n. 7; P.L., 183:866-D.

speculation, an intellectual diversion, fascinating the mind with its play of light and glory, but it is moved, impelled, and governed by love. Wherefore, borne up by this wisdom and by means of meditation, contemplation, and love, Bernard ascends the peak of the mystical life and is united with God Himself, tasting at times almost infinite happiness even in this mortal life.

His style, which is animated, rich, smooth, and characterized by vivid language, is filled with such pleasing unction that it attracts, delights and raises to heavenly things the mind of the reader. It arouses, nourishes and strengthens piety; it spurs the soul to the pursuit of those good things which are not passing or transitory, but true, certain, and everlasting. For this reason, his writings were always held in high honor. And from them the Church herself has inserted into the Sacred Liturgy not a few pages redolent of heaven and breathing forth the fire of piety.[11] They seem to have been nourished with the breath of the Divine Spirit, and to shine with a light so resplendent that the course of the centuries is unable to extinguish it, since it comes forth from the soul of a writer longing after truth and love, and yearning to nourish others and to conform them to his own image.[12]

It is a pleasure, Venerable Brethren, for the edification of all, to quote some fine passages, from his works, on this mystical teaching: "We have taught that every soul, even though weighed down with

[11] *Cfr. Brev. Rom.*
[12] *Cfr.* Fenelon, *Panegyrique de St. Bernard.*

sins, ensnared in vice, caught in the allurements
of the passions, held captive in exile, and imprisoned
in the body . . . even, I say, though it be thus
damned and in despair, can find within itself not
only reasons for yearning after the hope of pardon
and the hope of mercy, but also for making bold to
aspire to marriage with the Word, not hesitating to
establish a covenant of union with God, and not
being ashamed to be yoked in one sweet bond of love
along with the King of the Angels. What will the soul
not dare with Him whose marvelous image it sees
within itself, and whose striking likeness it recognizes
in itself?" [13] "By this conformity of charity . . . the
soul is wedded to the Word, when, namely, loving
even as she is loved, she exhibits herself in her will
conformed to Him to Whom she is already conformed in her nature. Therefore, if she loves Him perfectly she has become His Bride. What can be more
sweet than such a conformity? What can be more
desirable than this charity, whereby thou art enabled
of thyself to draw nigh with confidence to the Word,
to cleave to Him steadfastly, to interrogate Him famil-
iarly, and to consult Him in all thy doubts, as
audacious in thy desires as thou art capacious in thy
understanding? This is in truth the alliance of holy and
spiritual marriage. But it is too little to call it an
alliance: it is rather an embrace. Surely we have then a
spiritual embrace when the same likes and the same
dislikes make one spirit out of two. Nor is there any

[13] *In Cantica,* Sermon 83, n. 1; P.L., 183:1181-C, D.

occasion to fear lest the inequality of the persons should cause some defect in the harmony of wills, since love knows nothing of reverence. Love means an exercise of affection, not an exhibition of honor. . . . Love is all-sufficient for itself. Whithersoever love comes, it subjugates and renders captive to itself all the other affections. Consequently, the soul that loves, simply loves and knows nothing else except to love." [14]

After pointing out that God wants to be loved by men rather than feared and honored, he adds this wise and penetrating observation: "Love is sufficient of itself; it pleases of itself, and for its own sake. It counts as merit to itself and is its own reward. Besides itself love requires no motive and seeks no fruit. Its fruit is its enjoyment of itself. I love because I love, and I love for the sake of loving. A great thing is love, if yet it returns to its Principle, if it is restored to its Origin, if it finds its way back again to its Fountainhead, so that it may be thus enabled to continue flowing with an unfailing stream. Amongst all the emotions, sentiments, and feelings of the soul, love stands distinguished in this respect, that in this one case alone has the creature the power to correspond and to make a return to the Creator in kind, though not in equality." [15]

Since in his prayer and his contemplation he had frequently experienced this divine love, whereby we can be intimately united with God, there broke forth

14 *Ibid.*, n. 3; P.L., 183:1182-C, D.
15 *Ibid.*, n. 4; P.L., 183:1183-B.

from his soul these inspired words: "Happy is the Soul to whom it has been given to experience an embrace of such surpassing delight! This spiritual embrace is nothing else than a chaste and holy love, a love sweet and pleasant, a love perfectly serene and perfectly pure, a love that is mutual, intimate, and strong, a love that joins two, not in one flesh, but in one spirit, that makes two to be no longer two but one undivided spirit, according to the testimony of St. Paul,[16] where he says, 'He who cleaves to the Lord is one spirit with Him.' " [17]

In our day this sublime teaching of the Doctor of Clairvaux on the mystical life, which exceeds and can satisfy all human desires, seems sometimes to be neglected and relegated to a secondary place, or even forgotten by many who, completely taken up with the worries and business of daily life, seek and desire only what is useful and profitable for this mortal life, almost never lift their eyes and minds to heaven, and almost never aspire after heavenly things and values that cannot perish.

Yet, although not all can attain the summit of that exalted contemplation of which Bernard speaks with sublime words and sentences, and although not all can unite themselves so closely with God as to feel themselves linked in a mysterious manner with the Supreme Good through the bonds of heavenly marriage; nevertheless, all can and must from time to time lift their hearts from the earthly things around

[16] Cf. I Corinthians 6:17.
[17] *In Cantica*, Sermon 83, n. 6; P.L., 183:1184-c.

them to those of heaven, and most earnestly love the Supreme Giver of all good things.

Wherefore, since love for God is gradually growing cold today in the hearts of many, or is even not infrequently utterly extinct, we feel that these writings of the Mellifluous Doctor should be attentively meditated; because from their content, which for that matter comes from the Gospels, a new and heavenly force can pour forth, both into individual and into social life, in order to guide morality, make it conform with Christian precepts, and thus be able to provide timely remedies for the many great evils now troubling and attacking society. For when men do not have the proper love for their Creator, from Whom comes everything they have; when they do not love one another, then, as often happens, they are separated from one another by hatred and deceit and turn upon one another in bitter conflict. But God is the most loving Father of us all, and we are all brethren in Christ, we whom He redeemed by shedding His Precious Blood. Hence, as often as we fail to return God's love or reverently to recognize His divine fatherhood, the bonds of brotherly love are sundered in disaster and—as alas so often happens—discord, contention, and enmity burst out with tragic effects, going so far as to undermine and destroy the very foundations of human society.

Hence, that divine love which burned so mightily in the Doctor of Clairvaux must be re-enkindled in the hearts of all men, if we desire the restoration of Christian morality, if the Catholic religion is to carry out its mission successfully, and if, through the calming of dissension and the restoration of order in justice and equity, serene peace is to shine forth for a worn and anguished humanity.

May those who have embraced the Order of the Mellifluous Doctor, and all the members of the clergy, whose special task it is to exhort and urge others to the fervor of divine love, be most ardently inflamed with that love which ought always to unite us most perfectly with God. In our own day, more than at any other time—as we have said—men need this divine love; family life needs it; the whole of human society needs it. Where it burns and urges souls on to God, Who is the supreme goal of all mortals, all other virtues wax strong; when, on the contrary, it is absent or has died out, then tranquillity, peace, joy, and all other genuine good things gradually disappear or are completely destroyed, since they flow from Him who "is love." [18]

Of this divine charity no one, perhaps, has spoken more excellently, more profoundly, or more ardently than Bernard: "The reason for loving God," as he says, "is God; the measure of this love is to love without measure." [19] "Where there is love, there is no labor, but delight." [20] He admits having experienced this love himself when he writes: "O holy and chaste love! O sweet and comforting affection! . . . It is the more comforting and more sweet, the more the whole

[18] I *Ioan.*, 4, 8.
[19] *De Diligendo Deo*, c. 50; P.L., 182:974-A.
[20] *In Cantica*, Sermon 85, n. 8; P.L., 183:1191-D.

of that which is experienced is divine. To have such love, means being made like God." [21] And elsewhere: "It is good for me, O Lord, to embrace Thee all the more in tribulation, to have Thee with me in the furnace of trial rather than to be without Thee, even in heaven." [22] But when he touches upon that supreme and perfect love whereby he is united with God Himself in intimate wedlock, then he enjoys a happiness and a peace, than which none other can be greater: "O place of true rest . . . For we do not here behold God either, as it were, excited with anger, or as if distracted with care; but His will is proved to be 'good and acceptable and perfect.' This vision soothes instead of terrifying. It lulls to rest, instead of arousing, our unquiet curiosity. It calms the mind instead of fatiguing it. Here is found perfect repose. The tranquillity of God tranquillizes all about Him, and the contemplation of His rest is rest to the soul." [23]

However, this perfect quiet is not the death of the mind but its true life. ". . . Instead of bringing darkness and torpor, the sleep of the Spouse is wakeful and life-giving; it illuminates the mind, drives out the death of sin, and bestows immortality. Nevertheless, it is a true sleep, which transports rather than stupefies the faculties. It is also a true death. This I affirm without the least hesitation, since the Apostle says, in commendation of some who were still living

[21] *De Diligendo Deo*, c. 10, n. 28; P.L., 182:991-A.
[22] In Ps. 90, Sermon 18, n. 4; P.L., 183:252-C.
[23] *In Cantica*, Sermon 23, n. 16; P.L., 183:893-A, B.

in the flesh,[24] 'You are dead, and your life is hid with Christ in God.' " [25]

This perfect tranquillity of mind, in which we enjoy the loving God by returning His love, and by which we turn and direct ourselves and all we have to Him, does not reduce us to laziness, sloth and inertia, but awakens an assiduous, efficient and active zeal that spurs us on to procure our own salvation and, with the help of God, that of others also. For this exalted contemplation and meditation, actuated and impelled by divine love, "regulates the affections, directs the actions, cuts away all excesses, forms character, orders and ennobles life, and lastly . . . endows the understanding with a knowledge of things divine and human. It . . . distinguishes what is confused, unites what is divided, collects what is scattered, discovers what is concealed, searches out what is true, examines what is probable, exposes what is false and deceptive. It . . . preordains what we have to do, and passes in review what has been accomplished, so that nothing disordered may remain in the mind, nor anything requiring correction. It . . . finally . . . makes provision for adversity, and thus endures misfortune, as it were, without feeling it, of which the former is the part of prudence, and the latter the function of fortitude." [26]

And in fact, although he longs to remain fixed in this most exalted and sweet contemplation and medi-

---

[24] *Col.*, 3, 3.
[25] *In Cantica*, Sermon 52, n. 3; P.L., 183:1031-A.
[26] *De Consideratione*, Bk. I, c. 7; P.L., 182:737-A, B.

tation, which is nourished by the Spirit of God, the Doctor of Clairvaux does not remain confined within the walls of his cell that "waxes sweet by being dwelled in" [27] but is at hand with counsel, word and action wherever the interests of God and Church are at stake. For he was wont to observe that "no one ought to live for himself alone, but all for all." [28] And moreover he said of himself and his monks: "In like manner, the laws of fraternity and of human society give our brethren, amongst whom we live, a claim upon us for counsel and assistance." [29] When with sorrowing mind he beheld the holy faith endangered or troubled, he spared neither labors, nor journeyings, nor any manner of pains to come stoutly to its defense, or to bring it whatever assistance he could. "I do not regard any of the affairs of God," he said, "as things in which I have no concern." [30] And to King Louis of France he penned these spirited words: "We sons of the Church cannot on any account overlook the injuries done to our mother, and the way in which she is despised and trodden under foot. . . . We will certainly make a stand and fight even to death, if need be, for our mother with the weapons allowed us; not with shield and sword, but with prayers and lamentations to God." [31]

To Abbot Peter of Cluny he wrote: "And I glory in tribulations if I have been counted worthy to en-

[27] *De Imit. Christi*, I, 20, 5.
[28] *In Cantica*, Sermon 41, n. 6; P.L., 183:987-B.
[29] *De adventu D.*, Sermon 3, 5; P.L., 183:45-D.
[30] *Epist.* 20 (*ad Card. Haimericum*); P.L., 182:123-B.
[31] *Epist.* 221, 3; P.L., 182:386-D, 387-A.

dure any for the sake of the Church. This, truly, is my glory and the lifting up of my head: the triumph of the Church. For if we have been sharers of her troubles, we shall be also of her consolation. We must work and suffer with our mother. . . ." [32]

When the mystical body of Christ was torn by so grave a schism that even good men on both sides became heated in conflict, he bent all his efforts to settling disagreements and happily restoring unity of mind. When princes, led by desire of earthly dominion, were divided by fearful enmity, and the welfare of nations was thereby seriously threatened, he was ever the arbiter of peace and the architect of mutual accord. When, finally, the holy places of Palestine, hallowed by the blood of our Divine Savior, were threatened with gravest danger, and were hard pressed by foreign armies, at the command of the Supreme Pontiff with loud voice and still farther-reaching charity he roused Christian princes and peoples to undertake a new crusade; and if indeed it was not brought to a successful conclusion, the fault was surely not his.

And above all, when the integrity of Catholic faith and morals, the sacred heritage handed down by our forefathers, was jeopardized especially by the activities of Abelard, Arnold of Brescia and Gilbert de la Porée, strong in the grace of God he spared no pains in composing books replete with the deepest wisdom and making laborious journeys, that errors might be

[32] *Epist.* 147, 1; P.L., 182:304-C, 305-A.

dispelled and condemned, and that the victims of error might as far as possible be recalled to the straight path and to virtuous living.

But since he was well aware that in matters of this kind the authority of the Roman Pontiff prevails over the opinions of learned men, he took care to introduce that authority which he recognized as supreme and infallible in settling such questions. To his former discipline, our predecessor of blessed memory Eugene III, he wrote these words which reflect at once his exceeding great love and reverence and that familiarity which becomes the saints: "Parental love knows nothing of lordship; it recognizes not a master but a child even in him who wears the tiara. . . . Therefore shall I admonish thee now, not as a master, but as a mother, yea, as a most loving mother." [33]

Then he addresses him with these powerful words: "Who art thou? Thou art the High Priest and the Sovereign Pontiff. Thou art the Prince of pastors and the Heir of the apostles . . . by thy jurisdiction, a Peter; and by thy unction, a Christ. Thou art he to whom the keys have been delivered and the sheep entrusted. There are indeed other gatekeepers of heaven, and there are other shepherds of the flock; but thou art in both respects more glorious than they in proportion as thou hast inherited a more excellent name. They have assigned to them particular portions of the flock, his own to each; whereas thou art given charge of all the sheep, as the one Chief Shep-

[33] *De Consideratione,* Prologue; P.L., 182:727-A, 728-A, B.

herd of the whole flock. Yea, not only of the sheep, but of the other pastors also art thou the sole supreme Shepherd." [34] And again: "He who wishes to discover something which does not appertain to thy charge will have to go outside the world." [35]

In clear and simple fashion he acknowledges the infallible magisterium of the Roman Pontiff in questions of faith and morals. For recognizing the errors of Abelard, who when he "speaks of the Trinity savors of Arius; when of grace, of Pelagius; when of the person of Christ, of Nestorious," [36] "who . . . predicated degrees in the Trinity, measure in majesty, numbers in eternity"; [37] and in whom "human reason usurps for itself everything and leaves nothing for faith"; [38] he not only shatters, weakens and refutes his subtle, specious and fallacious tricks and sophisms, but also on this subject writes to our predecessor of immortal memory Innocent II these words of utmost importance: "Your See should be informed of all dangers that may arise, especially those that touch on faith. For I consider it meet that damage to the faith be repaired in the particular place where faith is perfectly whole. These indeed are the prerogatives of this See. . . . It is time, most loving Father, that you recognized your pre-eminence. Then do you really take the place of Peter, whose See you hold, when by your admonition you confirm hearts weak in

[34] *Ibid.*, Bk. II, c. 8; P.L., 182:751-C, D.
[35] *Ibid.*, Bk. III, c. 50; P.L., 182:757-B.
[36] *Epist.* 192; P.L., 182:358-D, 359-A.
[37] *Contra Errores Abaelardi*, I, 2; P.L., 182:1056-A.
[38] *Epist.* 188; P.L., 182:353-A, B.

faith, when by your authority you break the corrupters of the faith." [39]

But whence this humble monk with hardly any human means at his disposal was able to draw the strength to overcome difficulties of the most arduous kind, to settle the most intricate questions, and to solve the most troublesome cases, can only be understood when one considers the exalted sanctity of life which distinguished him, and his great zeal for truth. For, as we have said, he was above all on fire with a most burning charity toward God and his neighbor (which, as you know, Venerable Brethren, is the chief and as it were all-embracing commandment of the Gospel), so that he was not only united to the heavenly Father by uninterrupted mystical union, but desired nothing more than to win men to Christ, to uphold the most sacred rights of the Church, and to defend with all his heart the integrity of the Catholic faith.

Although he was held in great favor and esteem by popes, princes and peoples, he was not puffed up, he did not grasp at the vain, fleeting glory of men, but ever shone with that Christian humility which "acquires other virtues . . . having acquired them, keeps them . . . keeping them, perfects them"; [40] so that "without it the others do not even seem to be virtues." [41] Wherefore "proferred honor did not tempt his soul, nor did he set his foot on the down-

[39] *Contra Errores Abaelardi, Praef.*; P.L., 182:1053-1054-D.
[40] *De moribus et off. Episc., seu Epist.*, 42, 5, 17; P.L., 182:821-A.
[41] *Ibid.*

ward path of worldly glory; tiara and ring had no
more appeal for him than rake or hoe." [42] And while
he undertook such great and frequent labors for the
glory of God and the benefit of the Christian name,
he was wont to call himself "the useless servant of
the servants of God," [43] "a vile worm," [44] "a tree without fruit," [45] "a sinner, ashes. . . ." [46] This Christian
humility, as well as the other virtues, he nourished by
assiduous contemplation of heavenly things, and by
fervent prayer to God, by which he called down
grace from on high on the labors undertaken by himself and his followers.

So ardent was the love he bore in a special manner
to Jesus Christ Our Divine Savior that under its influence and inspiration he penned the fine and profound pages which still arouse the admiration and
enkindle the devotion of all readers. "What can so
enrich the soul that reflects upon it [the holy name
of Jesus]? What can . . . fortify the virtues, en-
gender good and honorable dispositions, foster holy
affections? Dry is every kind of spiritual food, which
this oil does not moisten. Insipid, whatever this salt
does not season. If thou writest, thy composition has
no charms for me, unless I read there the name of
Jesus. If thou disputest or conversest, I find no pleasure in thy words, unless I hear there the name of
Jesus. Jesus is honey in the mouth, melody in the ear,

[42] *Vita Prima,* II, 25; P.L., 185:283-B.
[43] *Epist.* 37; P.L., 182:143-B.
[44] *Epist.* 215; P.L., 182:379-B.
[45] *Vita Prima,* V, 12; P.L., 185:358-D.
[46] *In Cantica,* Sermon 71, n. 5; P.L., 183:1123-D.

a cry of joy in the heart. Yet not only is that name light and food. It is also medicine. Is any amongst you sad? Let the name of Jesus enter his heart; let it leap thence to his lips; and lo! the light that radiates from that name shall scatter every cloud and restore tranquillity. Has someone sinned, and is he, moreover, abandoning hope, rushing in desperation toward the snare of death? Let him but invoke this life-giving name, and straightway he shall experience a renewal of courage. . . . Whoever, when trembling with terror in the presence of danger, has not immediately felt his spirits revive and his fears departing as soon as he called upon this name of power? . . . There is nothing so efficacious as the name of Jesus for restraining the violence of anger, repressing the swellings of pride, healing the smarting wound of envy. . . ." [47]

To this fervent love for Jesus Christ was joined a most sweet and tender devotion toward His glorious Mother, whose maternal love he repaid with filial affection, and whom he jealously honored. So great was his confidence in her most powerful intercession that he did not hesitate to write: "It is the will of God that we should have nothing which has not passed through the hands of Mary." [48] Likewise: "Such is the will of God, Who would have us to obtain everything through the hands of Mary." [49]

And here it is well, Venerable Brethren, to pro-

[47] *In Cantica,* Sermon 15, n. 6; P.L., 183:846-D, 847-A, B.
[48] *In vigil. Nat. Domini,* Sermon 3, n. 10; P.L., 183:100-A.
[49] *Sermon in Nat. Mariae,* 7; P.L., 183:441-B.

pose to the consideration of all a page in praise of
Mary than which there is perhaps none more beautiful, more impassioned, more apt to excite love for
her, more useful for stirring devotion and inspiring
imitation of her virtuous example: "Mary . . . is interpreted to mean 'Star of the Sea' and admirably
suits the Virgin Mother. There is indeed a wonderful appropriateness in this comparison of her to a
star, because as a star sends out its rays without
detriment to itself, so did the Virgin bring forth her
Child without injury to her integrity. And as the ray
emitted does not diminish the brightness of the star,
so neither did the Child born of her tarnish the
beauty of Mary's virginity. She is therefore that glorious star, which, according to prophecy, arose out of
Jacob, whose ray illumines the entire earth, whose
splendor shines out conspicuously in heaven and
reaches even unto hell. . . . She, I say, is that resplendent and radiant star, placed as a necessary
beacon above life's great and spacious sea, glittering
with merits, luminous with examples for our imitation. Oh, whosoever thou art that perceivest thyself
during this mortal existence to be rather floating in
the treacherous waters, at the mercy of the winds
and the waves, than walking secure on the stable
earth, turn not away thine eyes from the splendor of
this guiding star, unless thou wishest to be submerged
by the tempest! When the storms of temptation
burst upon thee, when thou seest thyself driven upon
the rocks of tribulation, look up at the star, call upon
Mary. When buffeted by the billows of pride, or

ambition, or hatred, or jealousy, look up at the star, call upon Mary. Should anger, or avarice, or carnal desires violently assail the little vessel of thy soul, look up at the star, call upon Mary. If troubled on account of the heinousness of thy sins, confounded at the filthy state of thy conscience, and terrified at the thought of the awful judgment to come, thou art beginning to sink into the bottomless gulf of sadness and to be absorbed in the abyss of despair, oh, then think of Mary. In dangers, in doubts, in difficulties, think of Mary, call upon Mary. Let not her name depart from thy lips, never suffer it to leave thy heart. And that thou mayest more surely obtain the assistance of her prayer, neglect not to walk in her footsteps. With her for guide, thou shalt never go astray; whilst invoking her, thou shalt never lose heart; so long as she is in thy mind, thou art safe from deception; whilst she holds thy hand, thou canst not fall; under her protection, thou hast nothing to fear; if she walks before thee, thou shalt not grow weary; if she shows thee favor, thou shalt reach the goal." [50]

We can think of no better way to conclude this encyclical letter than with the words of the Mellifluous Doctor to invite all to practice an ever-growing devotion to the loving Mother of God, and according to their respective state in life to imitate diligently her exalted virtues. If at the beginning of the twelfth century grave dangers threatened the Church and human society, the imminent perils of our own age

[50] *Hom. II super "Missus est,"* 17; P.L., 183:70-B, C, D, 71-A.

are hardly less formidable. The Catholic faith, supreme solace of mankind, often languishes in souls, and in many regions and countries is even subjected to the bitterest public attacks. With the Christian religion either neglected or cruelly destroyed, public and private morals, alas, are seen to stray from the straight way, and often over the tortuous windings of error to end miserably in vice.

Charity, which is the bond of perfection, concord and peace, is replaced by hatred, enmities and discords.

A certain restlessness, anxiety and fear have invaded the minds of men; it is truly to be greatly feared that if the light of the Gospel gradually abates and fades in the minds of many, or if—what is even worse—they utterly reject it, the very foundations of civil and domestic society will collapse, and worse and more tragic times will follow.

Therefore as the Doctor of Clairvaux sought and obtained from the Virgin Mother Mary help for the troubles of his times, let us all through the same great devotion and prayer so strive to move our divine Mother that she may obtain from God timely relief from these grave evils which have either already come upon us or may yet befall, and that she who is benign and most powerful will by the help of God grant that the sincere, solid and fruitful peace of the Church may at last dawn on all nations and peoples.

Such be, through the intercession of Bernard, the rich and salutary effects of the centenary celebration of his most holy death. Let all join us in prayer for this intention, while, studying and meditating on the example of the Mellifluous Doctor, they strive earnestly and eagerly to follow in his footsteps.

As a pledge of these salutary fruits, we bestow with heartfelt affection our Apostolic Blessing upon you, Venerable Brothers, upon the flocks committed to your care and in a special manner on those who have entered Saint Bernard's own Order.

Given at Rome in Saint Peter's, on the Feast of Pentecost, the twenty-fourth day of May of the year MCMLIII, the fifteenth of our pontificate.

POPE PIUS XII

BIBLIOGRAPHY
AND INDEX

Bernardi, Sancti, *Opera Omnia,* in Migne, *Patrologia Latina,* Vols. 182-185
Bernard, P., moine de Sept Fons, *Saint Bernard et Notre Dame* (anthology), Paris, 1953
Chatillon, Jean, ed., *Prière et Union à Dieu, Textes de S. Bernard,* Paris, 1953
Commission d'Histoire de l'Ordre de Citeaux, *Bernard de Clairvaux,* Paris, 1953
Dictionnaire de Spiritualité, Paris, 1932
Dimier, P. Anselme, moine de Chimay, *Saint Bernard, Pêcheur de Dieu,* Paris, 1953
Dumontier, P. Maurice, moine de Chimay, *Saint Bernard et la Bible,* Paris, 1953
Gilson, Etienne, *The Mystical Theology of Saint Bernard,* New York, 1940
——, *The Spirit of Medieval Philosophy,* New York, 1936
——, *Saint Bernard, Textes Choisis,* Paris, 1949
James, Bruno Scott, trans., *The Letters of Saint Bernard of Clairvaux,* Chicago, 1953
Leclercq, Dom Jean, *Saint Bernard Mystique,* Paris, 1948
Luddy, Fr. Ailbe, monk of Mount Melleray, *The Life and Times of Saint Bernard,* Dublin, 1927
Roschini, P. Gabriele, *Il Dottore Mariano,* Rome, 1953
Temoignages, "Cahiers de la Pierre Qui Vire," *Saint Bernard, Homme d'Église,* Paris, 1953
Vacandard, Abbé, *Vie de Saint Bernard,* Paris, 1910
William of Saint Thierry, *Vita Sancti Bernardi,* Migne, P.L., Vol. 184
Williams, Watkin, *Saint Bernard of Clairvaux,* Manchester, England, 1953
——, *Saint Bernard, The Man and His Measure,* Manchester, England, 1944

Index

Index

40687